25 WAYS

Women

Can Motivate
Themselves

STACIA PIERCE

1st Printing

25 Ways Women Can Motivate Themselves
ISBN: 1-886880-19-0
Copyright © 1998 by Stacia Pierce
Published by Life Changers Publishing
808 Lake Lansing Rd. Ste. 200
East Lansing, MI 48823

TABLE OF CONTENTS

PART III: SPIRITUAL MOTIVATION

DEDICATION

It gives me great pleasure to dedicate this book to my wonderful husband James and our two children: Ariana and Ryan. You all are a great source of motivation to my life and the success of it.

To James, thanks for motivating me to fulfill my dreams.

To Ariana, thanks for motivating me to live a life of fun and laughter.

To Ryan, thanks for motivating me to treasure motherhood and the joy of building a rich family heritage.

Acknowledgements

My heartfelt appreciation is expressed to Sharlette Marshall, Sabrina Todd, Daphine Whitfield, The Women's Leadership Team, Women in The Word supporters and the Life Changers Christian Center Family. I would also like to thank those supporters throughout the country who participated in my seminars or conferences and requested a book such as this one.

INTRODUCTION

Motivation: A reason for action and a necessary ingredient to living a successful life. I believe without a doubt that continued motivation is God's will for you. He wants you to be motivated all the time.

To be a motivated person means you are self-confident, energetic, full-spirited, optimistic, positive, imaginative, exciting, objective and successful. Wow, what a wonderful way to experience life!

As a result of reading this book you will have the tools you need to be personally and permanently motivated. You will learn how to encourage and energize yourself and others to reach new levels of success.

PART I
PHYSICAL
MOTIVATION

#1
Smile

"Whoever is happy will make others happy too."
-Anne Frank

A smile is an expression that says that I'm pleased, happy and proud. I once read a book that said that the first forty seconds you see a person, sets the tone for the rest of your time together. That statement stayed with me and caused me to alter my attitude. I wake up in the morning and consciously put a smile on my face.

I began the practice of smiling at my husband and beginning each day by saying some encouraging words. I smile at my children first thing in the morning and tell them how blessed their day is going to be. A smile can alter someone else's mood not to mention your own. Psychological tests prove that when you are smiling you feel better.

Each day I make it a point to smile while giving sincere compliments to my famliy. This makes the atmosphere in our home more pleasant and enjoyable. A smile is contagious. When you smile at someone, they normally return the gesture and your spirit is lifted. It's automatic. Similar to a compliment, a heartfelt smile makes the other person feel better about themselves.

A smile sends positive words out of your mouth. Have you ever seen pessimistic talk come through a genuine smile? Of course not. Go ahead, smile. A happy, motivated person wears a smile. It's much easier than frowning. Fourteen muscles are needed to frown and only seven to smile. As you begin to wear a smile, the complementing actions will follow.

Zig Ziglar wrote a book called, *Something to Smile About*. The entire book gives illustrations to show how you can find *something* to smile about in your everyday life. I have a quote in my bathroom that says; "A smile happens quickly, but the memory of it lasts a long time." It's true. I still remember those smiles of approval and applause from my parents.

They were so important to my self-confidence.
At thirteen years old, I had to model before a
large audience for the first time. I was the
youngest in the group and I was very nervous.
Timidly, I looked in the audience and saw my
father smiling and nodding his head. Instantly
the nervousness faded away.

Surrounding yourself with things that make you
smile: a bouquet of flowers, your family photo
album or inspirational cards or posters. Hang
your awards around the office or hang your
children's photographs in the family room.

Usually happy people smile. Have you made a
decision to be happy? I believe that happiness
is a decision.

There will be trials in our lives that sadden us,
but we do not have to remain in a sorrowful
state of mind. We must all make an effort to
move on, because life has so many rewards
awaiting us.

Life improves as we learn to continuously renew our minds to the word of God. Seek the truth and look for beauty and good in our day-to-day situations. We have to learn to add joy to our own lives and not wait for someone else to give it to us.

My daughter Ariana just recently had a birthday party. She spent the majority of the day excited and smiling in anticipation of her party. My observation of Ariana made me think how the art of celebration makes our lives richer and more enjoyable. If you want to make yourself smile, don't wait until your birthday to have a party. Invite a few friends over for dessert, tea and games. Just the preparation will make you smile. Practice smiling even when you're alone. Read a book or watch a funny movie.

Recently, I went through a stack of cards and letters I received from women who have enjoyed listening to my tapes and reading my books. The testimonies of how their lives have been changed, along with their encouraging words caused me to smile and laugh. Dig through old cards and letters, remember the good times.

Most business owners understand how important a little smile can be. One of my friends used to work for a telemarketing firm. She told me how a major part of the training for telemarketing is based on attitude. These firms train their operators to smile at all times while talking on the phone. Statistics have proven that those who smile while on the phone have a much higher success ratio with clients. Isn't it amazing that smiling has a positive effect even when you can't see the person on the line?

Smiling is a powerful tool in living a successful life. You will attract a lot of people to you if you are a happy person who brightens a room by just entering it. The opposite is also true. You can repel people from you if you are the person who is so serious that the atmosphere dampens each time you enter a room.

I once counseled a young lady who was about to lose her job because her boss said she never smiled at work, and she seemed unhappy with her job. This was far from the truth; she enjoyed her work, she just never expressed it. I suggested that she alter her attitude and begin smiling and giving sincere compliments or appeciation to co-workers and her boss whenever opportunities arose. In just a few months, she was reviewed and told that she was an excellent worker and deserved a raise.

Begin to take notice of facial expressions. What are you projecting to those around you? Remember, whoever is happy makes others happy too. So smile more, it makes others wonder what you're up to. Share some enthusiasm and optimism with those around you. It's almost impossible to make someone else's day and not make your own in the process.

POINTS OF MOTIVATION

☞Smile at your spouse or children daily.

☞Before your next phone conversation, remember to smile. It will enhance your conversation.

☞When you are at the checkout counter paying for your groceries, smile at the cashier, you will brighten their day.

☞Include more activities in your life that will cause you to smile.

☞Do someone a favor, then bask in their gratitude.

☞Smile at God's beautiful creation, the flowers, the birds and their chirping, the rain hitting against the windows etc.

☞Put a mirror by your work station and look in it throughout your day as a reminder to smile.

☞Take an inventory of all the good things happening in your life right now. You may find that you have more to smile about than you think.

☞The next time you enter a room full of people enter with a smile on your face. They will probably be more apt to receive you.

☞Go to the mirror and look yourself in the eyes, smile and say, "I believe in you."

☞Make sure your bedroom is as pleasant and orderly as possible before you go to bed, so you'll wake up wanting to smile. It's harder to wake up smiling when you hate your surroundings.

☞Post up inspiring quotes throughout your house.

MY MOTIVATIONAL JOURNAL

Make yourself a list of what you can smile about this week.

What can you do to cultivate a smile habit?

How can you cause somebody to smile today?

#2
Laugh

"The most wasted of all days is that one on which one has not laughed."
-Sebastian Roche

Laugh every chance you get. A hearty belly laugh stimulates the release of chemicals in the brain that increase your motivation. The Bible tells us that a merry heart doeth good like a medicine. It encourages laughter. Recall the biblical story of Abraham and Sarah. Abraham was very old when God declared that they would bear a child. At first they burst into laughter, later Sarah bore a son. The child's name was Issac (which means laughter).

Laughing is one of the bodies best antidotes for anxiety. "A big belly laugh stretches the muscles from the diaphragm to the scalp releasing the tension that causes fatigue and headaches," [1]

23

It also boosts circulation and oxygen in the blood, giving you a burst of energy.

Many physical benefits of laughter have been studied and documented. In doing research for my book; *A Christian Woman's Guide to Health and Nutrition*, I found some motivating factors about laughter. A good chuckle can boost your immune system. It can also help to lower your blood pressure, lower your stress rate and improve the flow of blood to the brain. Other healthy benefits of laughter include the improvement of relationships, emotional stability, the ability to focus on your interests, an increase in your energy level, and it stimulates your creativity.

Learn to laugh at yourself, it will give you balance in life. Laughing at yourself doesn't mean belittling or putting yourself down. The key is to stay positive, don't become sarcastic or cynical. Learn to surround yourself with positive people who lift you up instead of negative people who put you down. When you are positive and practice laughing, you'll gain more friends and more opportunities to live the motivated life.

Thackey says, "A good laugh is sunshine in a house." At our house on family night, we sometimes rent a few funny videos and chuckle together. We also have a couple of board games we play that always fills the room with laughter. One of our favorites is MAD GAB™, where you have to sound out words or phrases to get the answer and win points. It sounds so silly to hear your teammates yelling trying desperately to hear the correct answer. Usually everyone laughs until they're breathless, it's great fun. The next time you're out shopping, browse through the game section and find some funny games to add to your family time and social gatherings.

Did you know that there was actually a society for ladies who laugh out loud? They are dedicated to locating the laughter in their lives, so they swap hilarious stories at monthly meetings. These ladies say that looking for the humorous side of life helps them to cope with stress. You may not want to form a society, but an organized laughing session is not a bad idea. Gather a bunch of your liveliest friends (or borrow someone else's) and do something that stimulates laughter. Focus on the benefits of laughter and you'll want to experience laughing everyday.

THE BENEFITS OF ADDING LAUGHTER TO YOUR LIFE:

☺ Laughter helps you enjoy life more.

☺ Laughter causes you to be more optimistic.

☺ Laughter restores your energy.

☺ Laughter stimulates your creativity.

☺ Laughter improves your relationships.

☺ Laughter helps you stay physically healthy and fight disease.

James S. Walsh said "people who laugh actually live longer than people who don't laugh." Few persons realize that health actually varies according to the amount of laughter one experiences in their life.

I love what Raymond Hitchcock says, "A man isn't poor if he can still laugh." Make an effort to look at the funny side of everything. Some have learned to make a living that way. Everyday find ways to add laughter to your life. Motivated, happy people have learned the art of living, loving and laughing.

POINTS OF MOTIVATION

☞ Play games with family and friends that make you laugh.

☞ Look for humor in everyday life.

☞ Read a humorous book.

☞ Schedule regular meeting times with friends who make you laugh.

☞ Call the person that always makes you laugh.

☞ Keep a tape of your favorite comedian in the car.

☞ Laugh daily. At the end of each day, think, did I laugh today?

☞ Share laughs with your friends, not sob stories.

☞ Learn not to take yourself so seriously when you blow it. Find humor in the situation and laugh out loud.

☞Make your home a happy place to be. Allow your children the freedom to laugh and be silly at times.

"Let the children laugh and be glad. O my dear they haven't long before the world assaults them. Allow them genuine laughter now. Laugh with them, till tears run down your faces - till a memory of pure delight and precious relationship is established within them, indestructable, personal and forever."
-Unknown

☞Laugh with your mate, it'll keep your marriage healthy.

☞Buy cards that make others laugh.

☞Laugh alot in your bedroom, it will create favorable memories in the place you spend alot of your time.

☞Share a great joke.

MOTIVATIONAL JOURNAL

What do you do on a regular basis that causes you to laugh?

What are some of the ways you can choose to enjoy life more?

#3
Give Yourself
Away

*"You'll always have everything in life you want if
you help enough other people get what they want."*
-Zig Ziglar

The Bible tells us clearly in I Peter 4:9 to share
our homes with those who need a meal or a
place to stay for a night. Being hospitable is
an excellent way to give yourself away. I consider myself a "people person." Every opportunity I get, I open my home to friends and
family for a special time of sharing.

One Labor Day we had a backyard barbecue
and invited several friends who didn't know one
another. The week before the event a game idea
came to me. I named it "The Game of Purpose." As the guests came in the door, they
were handed a slip of paper with the game instructions (Figure 1a). My guests were required

```
Name: John
Please find Jeff Doe and ask him what his purpose is.
Record here:_____

Tell him one thing you will do within the next month to help him in
accomplishing his purpose.
I will:_____
```

(Figure 1a)

to share one goal with their partner, and discuss how they could help one another achieve
their dreams. The game provoked so much joy
and laughter as different pairs excitedly sat
down to share about their desires and what they
were doing in life. No one wanted to stop sharing; you could hardly gather everyone to eat.

Over dessert my guests told me how thankful
they were that I gave myself away by taking the
time to bring so many people together for a
truly refreshing time of fellowship. During the
weeks following the party, I was encouraged
by the many thank you cards that poured in
from my friends.

My knack for coming up with games that con-
nect people surfaced again at one of my women's

leadership breakfast meetings hosted at my home. Each woman was given a previous assignment of observing for one month, and then writing twenty positive comments about one of the other women on the team they weren't especially familiar with.

That morning as the women sat in a circle they began to share with one another their positive observations. The tears began to flow, hugs were given, ministry took place and joy filled the hearts of everyone. Again I was encouraged and inspired by the impact that another instance of giving myself away had on my guests.

The purpose of giving yourself away is to make your guests feel special and loved. Don't just give yourself away to your guests, but offer this generosity to your family as well. Make your family feel special by adding flowers to the dinner table, putting a vase of fresh flowers in your children's room, or serving your husband breakfast in bed. Hospitality is just one way you can give yourself away, so be creative. Motivated people understand that the source of their energy comes from what they've given in the past.

Points of Motivation

☞Imagine all the ways you could share the best of who you are with someone else. These are a few that I came up with, but think of your own and give yourself away in special ways over the next 30 days.

☞Bake someone a cake or a dozen cookies and take it to them on a pretty platter.

☞Cook dinner for a friend with young children to give her a break.

☞Offer to baby-sit "free" for a friend while she does something fun.

☞Invite a friend over for lunch or dinner.

☞Decorate the dinner table with fresh flowers, candle light and your best dishes.

☞Give away encouraging words. Write an encouraging note to a friend.

☞Volunteer to help out at your church.

☞Make something for someone.

☞Read a book to your child

☞Fill a wicker basket with food and take it to someone who needs encouragement.

☞Host a party for no reason at all but to bring friends together.

☞Dedicate a day once a month to giving yourself to your children. Take them to the place or restaurant of their choice. Allow them to have a friend over.

☞Read *Silver Boxes* by Florence Littauer

☞Do something special for a friend or relative who may need a "pick me up." Take a short trip together (and you cover the cost). Or, pay for them to spend one night in a plush hotel while you babysit and allow them a day to themselves.

MY MOTIVATIONAL JOURNAL

*How do you feel about giving yourself away?
Explain.*

*What are a few of the things people have
done to give themselves away to you? How
did you feel?*

#4
Write Out
Your Vision

"Dare to dream...then turn your dreams into reality!"
-Cheryl Salem

The Bible tells us in Habakkuk: "Write the vision and make it plain." A vision in the mind is just an idea. It was once said that an idea is worth one dollar, but the plan for implementing the idea is worth a million. That's why it's essential that you write your vision on paper. I conducted a survey and asked women questions about their life's direction.

Most of the women who took the survey indicated that they were wandering aimlessly through life, merely surviving each day. These women said they spent their day raising children, tending to husbands, going to work or school and paying bills. All of them agreed that after a short period of time their daily routine becomes frustrating and demotivating.

You were created for achievement. God has a master plan for your success in life. It's time to take your Christianity a step further. Once you accept Jesus Christ as your Lord and Savior, and begin to get your mind renewed, you must also get your life renewed.

The Bible tells us that without a vision you will perish. Vision is your blueprint for life. Many women have shared with me that they feel like they are perishing. My response is usually, "create a vision." Vision is what causes you to wake up every morning excited about life, it gives you direction. There is something that you would love to do for life. The following questions should assist you in finding out what that something is.

Questions to Stir your Vision:
Write down your answer in a notebook labeled My Vision book.

✎What is the deepest desire of your heart?

✎What are you good at doing?

✎If no limitations existed (money, education, time), what would you really do with your life? Record it.

✎What flows naturally out of you?

✎What do mature Christians see in you? (You might want to ask your friends.)

✎What skills or gifts and talents do you have?

Reserve time to dream. Every once in a while, disconnect yourself from all activities and just dream. Try to schedule one day a month to be alone and review your vision. Because dreaming is unfamiliar to many of us, we shy away from it. God places dreams within us. He has great plans for our future. Everything God wants to do in your life will start as a thought or vision.

My dream of motivating ordinary women to live extraordinary lives began inside me long ago. It grew into the vision of Women of Royal

Destiny (W.O.R.D.) ministries which is our church's women's ministry. W.O.R.D. touches the lives of thousands of women on a consistent basis. My dream also grew into my becoming an author and motivational speaker at women's conferences. I could not escape my desire to help women. Finally I realized it was what the Lord had purposed for me to do.

Where is it that you want to end up in life? What dreams, visions or ideas are stirring on the inside of you? What is it that the Lord has purposed for you to do? Once you get your vision on paper, read it to yourself often. Begin to prepare yourself for opportunities that will arise in order for you to fulfill your vision.

MOTIVATIONAL POINTS

☞Reserve time to dream. Disconnect from your familiar surroundings. Take vacations, enjoy escape weekends, schedule "dream dates" with yourself in your planner.

☞Share your vision, your future plans with only those who will celebrate with you.

☞Put your vision down on paper, write it as creatively and expressively as possible. Keep it in a sacred place.

☞Make sure your future plans are inspiring.

☞Add photos to accompany your written vision.

☞Write out short term and long term goals that will lead you to accomplishing your vision.

My Motivational Journal

Do you know your vison well enough to communicate it?

What skills do you need to fulfill your vision? Write a list.

#5
Update your
Image

*"Not every woman in old slippers can manage to
look like Cinderella."*
-Don Marquis

Updating your image simply means that you've
decided you are important enough to look your
very best. You update by finding out what the
latest styles and colors are and then choosing
clothes, makeup, perfumes, and a new hair style
that fits your personal fashion style.

Style means more than just choosing clothes.
It's living with confidence. It's being content
with your choices. It's about reflecting the real
you in the way you dress, wear your hair and
accessorize. If you are going to stay motivated
about the way you look, then you will have to
develop a consistent routine of looking your

43

best. You may need to buy and read some books about developing your personal fashion style so you can educate yourself on what looks best on you. The book *Fabulous You* by Tori Hartman was one of my reading club books. The women who read it gave the book raving reviews, saying that it helped them develop a confident dressing style. Once you are secure about your personal style, all you have to do is consistently wear what looks good on you.

The Proverbs 31 woman was clothed in tapestries of scarlet and purple silks. These were very expensive and beautiful garments. In Exodus 28:2 (TLB) (when God appointed Aaron to indicate his separation to God) it says, "Begin to build a wardrobe of special clothes that will add dignity to your work." So even in the bible your appearance makes either a positive or negative impression.

When my husband and I do our marriage seminars, one of the main topics that men want addressed is on image upkeep for their wives. Men are attracted by sight. They are moved or motivated by what they see. So it is very important that a wife keeps herself visually appealing.

A good rule to apply is what I call the "remember me" rule. Don't allow your husband to see you looking frumpy when he leaves for work everyday, only to return from work to see you in the same tired state. There may be days that you aren't up when he leaves, or preparing for work yourself. But as a married woman, it's important to keep up your image for your husband - dress for him. If my husband and I aren't leaving the house together, I try to be groomed in a way that is pleasing for him to "remember me."

There are some common attitudes women have against image enhancement, which I address in my book, *Beauty the Inside Story*. A few of these attitudes bear to be addressed again.

Attitude #1 "I don't care about the way I look and what people think about me."

Response: This is a common attitude of people who have been hurt or rejected and don't want to put themselves in a position to be hurt or rejected again. Therefore, they want to make you think that your opinion of them doesn't matter.

The key is working from the inside out. Having confidence in who you are on the inside will help you to better reflect who you are on the outside. Improving the way you look is just an outward manifestation of an internal reality. You are a beautiful woman.

Attitude #2 "It's not worth the trouble, energy or money."

Response: That is an inability to see the benefit in making yourself the best possible you. Research shows that when you improve yourself, you become more effective in many areas of your life. Your self-esteem is boosted, more people are attracted to you and your income potential increases. You can't afford _not_ to improve your image.

The truth of the matter is, your clothes can really affect you. You begin to feel and become the way that you are dressed. Your appearance influences your emotions, So dress each day to communicate your dignity. You are beautiful, so put your best self forward everyday.

IMPROVE YOUR UNDERCOVER IMAGE:
Stop the fashion disasters that cause a negative self-image

☹ Wrong Deodorant/Antiperspirant

Are you really "sure?" Find one that works with your body chemistry to keep you dry and fresh. If you have bad odor problems, then see your doctor. Most stick deodorants leave white marks on your clothes, so I vote for roll-ons.

☹ Sagging or Wrong Color Nylons

Splurge and upgrade your brand or style of nylons. Search for stockings that match your

complexion and your figure. Wear comfortable nylons so you're not pulling and tugging
all day.

☹Unshaven Underarms

OOPS! What a fashion boo-boo, especially
when your arms are out. Did you know that
shaving also helps to decrease body odor?

☹The Bra

A lot of women suffer from bra problems. Get
fitted so you really know your right size. Find
a bra that lifts and gives the proper support.
Wear bras that accentuate your figure. Look
in a mirror and notice what your blouses and
shirts look like due to your choice of bra.

☹Your Monthly Cycle

Beware of body odors. You may need to bathe
twice a day during your cycle. Hint: Always
keep a little "freshen-up kit" in your purse containing extra sanitary supplies, baby wipes,

talcum powder etc. It's hard to function when you feel... not so fresh.

☹ Fragrance Needed

Studies have shown that women who wear fragrances such as powders, perfumes, body oils or lotions feel more confident about themselves. Getting dressed with fragrance is an uplifting way to start your day.

☹ Hairy Legs

The perfect way to mess up a lovely suit. If your legs get hairy, then shave them frequently, especially if you wear sheer nylons.

☹ Underwear Misfits

Throw out those torn and tight fitting underwear. Beautiful underwear will make you feel ten times better before you put your clothes on. Try to only wear matching sets. It's much more appealing than separates mixed and mismatched.

Image Solutions for Bedtime Beauty

❀ Invest in quality pajamas and appealing night clothes that are comfortable. Don't just throw on a beat up jogging suit or a big sweat shirt.

❀ A bubble bath or a steamy shower before bed is always relaxing. Adorn yourself with fragrant lotion and fresh scented powder. You'll sleep like a queen.

❀ Cleanse your face. Try not to leave makeup on overnight, it will cause your face to age faster. Give yourself a mini facial. After cleansing and toning, apply a night cream; you'll feel wonderful.

POINTS OF MOTIVATION

☞ Give yourself a facial.

☞ Brighten your wardrobe by adding some new accessories.

☞ Have your makeup done by a professional. Let her show you what colors look best on you and how to accentuate your best features.

☞ Take a closet inventory and give away every outfit you don't absolutely love to wear.

☞ Schedule an appointment to get a new haircut from a proven stylist.

☞ Keep a picture journal of your dream wardrobe. Collect photos from magazines and paste them in your Prayer and Purpose planner ora scrap book so you can visualize your personal style.

☞ Read, *Fabulous You* by Tori Hartman.

☞ Find and use a skin care system that works for you.

☞ Find yourself a signature fragrance.

☞ Browse a lingerie boutique to find new sleepwear.

☞ Discover your fashion style and dress the part.

☞ Write a list of image essentials you need to buy, i.e., bathing products, manicure set, new under garments, elegant nylons, etc.

☞ Always check the mirror before you leave the house.

☞ Paint your toenails.

MY MOTIVATIONAL JOURNAL

Describe how you look. What areas of your image are you most concerned about improving?

Outline the focus of your life with what kind of wardrobe you will need?

#6
Eat Healthy

*"The more raw fruits and veggies consumed,
especially veggies, the better off you are, the more
energy you'll consume."*
-Cheryl Townsley

Did you know that poor food choices produce poor health, and in the long run depletes your energy? Everything you put in your body affects everything you do. My eating habits as a child determined my health as an adult. I was raised in a household where beef was served twice a week. Each day we ate pork with breakfast and after dinner, dessert was a must. Although we had a small family of four, there was always enough food to feed a family of twelve. My friends loved to come to my house for dinner.

Due to my very active life-style, my weight was not a problem then. Consequently, I never paid attention to what I ate. Constant headaches, fatigue, colds and congestion were my usual burdens. Assuming they were normal, I missed the warning signs that my body was under serious attack, and disease was trying to get in.

At the point, where my headaches were more frequent and severe, I had an amazingly vivid dream. A monster chased me and I was running yelling, "Hypoglycemia, Hypoglycemia!" Awakening from the dream somewhat startled, I wrote the dream down and put away my journal.

Three years later, the symptom had disturbed me to the point where I consulted several doctors. Oddly, none of the doctors were able to diagnose my problem. In the midst of spending days running from one doctor to the next, my dream came back to my remembrance. Now I clearly understood what God was trying to show me. The disease called Hypoglycemia was chasing me and I couldn't keep running. It was time to turn around, face my health problems and confront the reality that it was time to eat differently.

Though I *thought* I ate healthy, my trip to the nutritionist proved otherwise. The nutritionist informed me that my illness was closely linked to foods I assumed were okay to eat. Case in point: chocolate chip cookies. They were my favorite treat and I baked them at least once a week, neglecting to realize that the sugar was destroying my immune system and sickness was beginning to destroy my life.

Sickness eats away at your life by consuming your time and depleting your energy. Ultimately, it will steal your motivation and your purpose if you allow it the opportunity.

RESTRUCTURE YOUR MEAL PLANNING

Meal planning will help you to achieve your goal of wholesome eating and eliminate bad practices. When you plan your meals you'll be less likely to wait until you're starving to eat. Searching for food in an extreme state of hunger will cause you to grab the quickest and usually the unhealthiest thing you can find. Just by implementing a few simple changes you can easily begin making healthy food choices.

Not only will you be encouraged, you will experience positive benefits from your new food choices. You'll experience a new level of energy. What are energy boosting foods? Fresh fruits and vegetables, seeds, whole grains, poultry, water, fish, and liver. Make vegetable, grains, legumes and fruits a major part of your daily diet. The following method will allow you the time to make healthy selections.

FOUR POINTS TO MEAL PLANNING

* Keep healthy low-fat snacks handy. Raisins, *Golden Temples* granola cereals, sunflower seeds, fresh fruit, carrots, celery sticks or raw nuts are goodies which are fun to eat

* Write out a schedule of what you will eat and chart when you will take your food breaks. Avoid going long periods of time without food.

* Keep fuel in your body all day long by eating several small snacks and meals. This way, you

can avoid hunger pangs which lead to negative food choices.

* When traveling bring your own snacks with you.

Meal planning motivates you to eat healthy by providing a strategy to keep your healthful eating goals consistent. Take a few minutes to sit down and plan your meals. You are worth the effort.

POINTS OF MOTIVATION

☞ Drink six to eight glasses of water a day. Buy 16 oz. bottles and keep one with you all day.

☞ Eat six small meals per day instead of three big ones.

☞ Refrain from processed foods such as canned, boxed or frozen dinners. They are un-natural and usually have no nutritional value.

☞ Limit your sugar intake. Sugar slows you down and produces a "yo-yo" effect in the blood sugar. Sugar ultimately drains you of energy.

☞ Add vitamins and herbal supplements to your daily diet. Vitamin E, C and A can be very beneficial to the overall health of women.

☞ Visit a health food store and buy books on health and nutrition. Also, inquire of the sales people which supplements would be helpful to you.

☞Learn to read labels. Check the ingredients in the food you buy. If mostly fats, oils and sugars are found at the beginning of the ingredients listing, then it's not good for you.

☞Try to give up meat for a few days a week. When you maintain a low fat, high fiber diet, you will have better digestion and reduce the risk of heart attacks.

☞Buy fresh fruits in season. Remember when shopping that processed foods usually have no nutritional value. The vitamins and other nutrients have been destroyed.

☞Create your own health library. Buy books that teach you about health and nutrition. Purchase quality healthy eating cookbooks so you can learn to prepare energy boosting foods.

MY MOTIVATIONAL JOURNAL

Start a food journal by recording everything you eat over the next month. It will help you lower your food intake and make healthier food choices.

What foods cause you to be tired within thirty minutes after consuming them? Make a list, and adjust the times in which you eat or avoid these items all together.

#7
Exercise

" We can do anything we want if we stick to
it long enough"
-Helen Keller

My advice is,...just do it! What is that you
say? You are not the exercising type? You
don't like to walk any further than from the car
to the front door? Well, here are a few motivational tips to help you renew your mind.

You owe it to yourself to just do it or at least
try. Your body is your responsibility and God
expects you to take care of it. Minimum exercise can greatly increase your health. It's a
guarantee that you will feel better if you walk
for at least thirty minutes, three days a week.
Studies show that a ten minute brisk walk increases mental and physical vigor. The body
and mind work together. For your mind to have
the same stamina to strive and be optimistic, your
body should be in the best shape possible.

Read magazines and books on exercise, health and fitness. You will be better equipped to determine which fitness plan works best for you. Did you know that once you get on a exercise program, you will naturally take on a more energetic life-style?

It is also a fact that people who exercise have a higher level of self-esteem than those who don't. Exercisers are more optimistic about their future.

To take your mind away from the fact that you are actually exercising, put on a pair of head phones and pop in your favorite teaching tape, audio book, or inspirational music cassette.

If you opt for walking as your method of exercise, but you hate to walk alone, form a walking club or grab a dependable friend.

For those of you who hate the outdoors, or are allergic to sunlight, your local mall could be your walking oasis. Most malls open their doors before normal operating hours to accommodate morning walkers. Health clubs or school facilities that have an indoor track are also good options. If your doctor has recommended that you not overexert yourself, call and ask him what he suggests for a fitness plan. Just don't feel like exercising? Renew your mind by reading the book of Proverbs where laziness is referenced often.

Become active. Get out more and go places. Enjoy the outdoors. The more active you become, the easier it will be to stick to a consistent exercise plan. How often should you exercise? Thirty minutes a day is good to start. Don't expect to do too much too frequently. Start slowly, but make it a goal to become a serious exerciser.

12 MOTIVATING REASONS TO GET UP & EXERCISE

✔ To increase your endurance

✔ To make you less susceptible to disease

✔ To strengthen your heart muscle

✔ To help you lose weight and keep it off

✔ To help prevent constipation

✔ To improve the quality of your sleep

✔ To increase self-esteem, confidence and a feeling of self-worth

✔ To relieve tension

✔ To help you handle stress more effectively

✔ To purify your blood

✔ To decrease cholesterol

✔ To relieve chronic fatigue and help you control your appetite

In order to actually put exercise in your schedule, you may have to make some sacrifices like, getting up early to work out before your family is awake. Maybe your schedule will permit a lunch time workout. Try bringing the kids along for a workout at the YMCA, and make exercise fun for the whole family.

Be flexible about the amount of time you spend exercising. Sometimes you may only be able to squeeze in thirty minutes. Other days you may be able to do a complete hour.

Also be flexible about the time of day you exercise. Whether you enjoy a morning or evening workout, there may be days that you have to adjust your schedule. Ask your friend or husband to watch the children while you exercise.

Don't put yourself on a strict exercise routine because you'll be more prone to give up. The emphasis should be on doing something you enjoy, but yet getting a workout, so you can maintain a healthy life-style.

POINTS OF MOTIVATION

☞Skip the elevators, take the stairs (unless you are in a hotel on the twentieth floor).

☞Next time you're grocery shopping, park away from the door.

☞Try a new sport (i.e. take tennis lessons).

☞Don't compare yourself to others.

☞Reward your efforts to get in shape with new workout clothes and shoes.

☞Cut out pictures of women exercising. Paste them in your Prayer and Purpose Planner and stay focused.

☞Read fitness magazines so that you are consistently learning about the benefits of exercise.

☞Buy some exercise equipment (if you're the type who will be committed to using it).

☞Dance or jump rope for about thirty minutes. Just move around if you can't find an entire workout.

☞Find an exercising partner to keep you motivated and keep you accountable to your goals.

☞If you can't find an exercise partner, go it alone.

☞Try exercising first thing in the morning. You'll start your day more alert and energized.

☞Exercise by playing ball with your children.

☞Buy his and hers bikes and exercise with your husband while you get in some personal time alone.

☞Aerobic exercise strengthens your heart and lungs, which in turn improves oxygen flow through your body and boosts your energy.

☞Next time you're doing housework, put on your gym shoes and jog up and down the stairs. Walk fast from one room to another and get your heart rate up.

MY MOTIVATIONAL JOURNAL

Describe your feelings about exercise?

Are you satisfied with your current body condition? If not what can you do to change it?

#8
Surround Yourself with Positive People

"The attitudes of positive people are contagious."
-Stacia Pierce

It is inevitable that the attitudes, mannerisms and beliefs of those around you will become your own; for better or worse. Who you associate with will directly affect how you feel. If your friends and associates are pessimistic people who always have negative conversations, you will eventually become de-motivated concerning your life. I've heard several testimonies of people whose lives drastically turned around towards success because of the input of just one positive person.

Sharlette works for my husband and I as a part

of the church staff. When she first joined the staff she was twenty-two years old and had been overweight all of her life and her self-image was shattered. She shared with us how the people she associated with frequently made negative comments about her weight.

My husband began to sow seeds of encouragement into her life. He told her that he believed she could be in excellent physical shape in a short period of time if she would just apply herself. In two years Sharlette lost over 60 lbs. and went from wearing a size 20 to wearing a size 12, all because she surrounded herself with positive people who spoke encouraging words to her.

Zig Ziglar says, "People have a way of becoming what you encourage them to be - not what you nag them to be." Bob Harrison says in his book, *Power Points for Success*, "If problem friends are stinking up your life, you have three options: 1. choose to continue the relationships 2. try to change the conditions it produces or; 3. separate yourself from the annoyance."

My husband and I have changed our friendships over the last five years because the people we were associated with were always going through some kind of crisis. They never had a positive report. Consequently, when we were optimistic about the future of our lives and ministry, they would literally get upset or jealous of us. One old friend thought it was her rightful duty to remind me that, "Everything wasn't always going to be good, so don't get too excited about where you are, or your future." When we made the choice to change our closest friends, our lives turned in a new direction, our ministry began to soar and our goals and dreams started manifesting right before our eyes.

I have found that the old cliche' "misery loves company" is a true. People who constantly walk around with a dreadful attitude would like for you to feel the same way they do. We eventually became like those with whom we associate.

My husband and I discovered that once we started being around positive people, we had greater faith to take on bigger projects.

After surrounding ourselves with positive people, our spirits and our outlook were raised.

Keep in touch with your positive friends, nurture those friendships. It's good to schedule regular luncheons with a motivating friend. Take mini-vacations together. If you are like me, most of your positive friends live far away. Keep in touch with them by letter writing or dropping an inspiring card in the mail. Update your friends on your success, and inquire about theirs. Nurture good relationships, it may not be easy, but it's necessary.

Remember, for you to stay motivated all the time, you must have access to people who are motivated all the time.

Over the past few years, I have collected some quotes I'd like to share with you from friends, books and magazines on positive friendships.

"A good friend is like a wonderful book. The inside is even better than the cover."
- Anonymous

"God chooses our relatives, we choose our friends"
-Jacques Delille

" A friend loves at all times."
-Proverbs 17:17

"One of the reasons we've survived our critics is that our friends helped keep us going."
-George Bush

"To be a winner you must associate with winners."
-Dexter Yager

"Those who bring sunshine to the lives of others cannot keep it from themselves."
-Anonymous

POINTS OF MOTIVATION

☞ Find positive things you can talk about with your friends, (i.e. a positive book article, a good report, audio cassette, etc.).

☞ Write down five positive things to share before your next meeting with a friend. This will keep your conversations pure, uplifting, and stimulating.

☞ Evaluate your closest associations in life, that's the direction you are headed. Do you want to continue to live like those you associate with?

☞ Keep a stack of inspirational cards on hand so it's convenient to drop a line to a friend when you think of them. Letter writing has become a lost art. Society has become so busy that we think we don't need meaningful relationships - that is until there is a crisis.

☞ If you read a good book, buy a copy and send it to a friend whom you think will benefit from it. Share wisdom and good information with your network of friends.

☞ Send photos of recent vacations or family events with a few lines to share your precious moments. Photos keep your relationships intimate and personal.

☞ Take vacations with your closest friends and embark on new experiences together.

☞ Be honest with your friends, there's no need for pretense. Be your true self and share your true thoughts. Advise a friend if you feel she is about to marry the wrong man, take the wrong job, or raise her children the wrong way. That's the beauty of friendship, you have someone who is outside of your household that truly cares about your well being.

☞ According to research from the United States, friendship is as important to keeping healthy as a balanced diet and regular exercise. Researchers believe it can boost the immune system and reduce the risk of illness like colds flu and even heart disease.

☞ When it comes to friends look for quality over quantity. A few good ones will give you all the support you need.

MY MOTIVATIONAL JOURNAL

*What kind of people do you have contact
with on a regular basis?*

*How do you feel after spending time with
your closest friends?*

#9
Beautify
Your Home

*"Your home should be a greenhouse where
you...flourish to your full potential."
-Vicki Kraft*

The atmosphere you create in your home directly affects your daily attitude. Beauty attracts. When your home is in disarray you want to avoid being there. When your home is visually appealing to you and your family, it will draw you there. Plus, your outlook on life is enhanced. A beautiful home will help you stay energized to enjoy life. You should create a home that helps you to be productive and happy.

You may need to start beautifying your home by cleaning it up. It's hard to have beauty without order. Go through each room of your house and make note of what needs to be cleaned up or cleared out. Then, establish a plan to clean one room at a time. When your house is out of order it will cause confusion, which is very de-motivating.

One of the ladies on my women's leadership team has small children whose hand prints always end up on the walls. So she touches up her walls with a fresh paint job about every six to nine months. It gives her house a clean orderly appearance.

Simply lighting up your house could be an instant beautifier. Light is invigorating and welcoming. A room with dim lighting can dampen the atmosphere.

I once went to an acquaintance's house who was suffering from minor depression. As I entered the house, the first thing I noticed was how dark and dim the house was. There were hardly any lights and, all of her furniture colors were brown, muted and earthy.

I suggested that she buy some lamps and brightly colored throw pillows to brighten up her house. She later admitted the lights helped to alter her mood tremendously.

The object of beautifying your home is decorating in a way that is pleasing to you and your family. Bright colors motivate me to think creatively. So the decor of my home inlcudes a lot of color. I couldn't find the colors I wanted to decorate my sun room, so I had two couches reupholstered and my kitchen chair seat covers made to match the couches. The room is so appealing and bright now that, the instant you walk in it, you smile and your spirit is lifted. Beauty can also be created with color.

Sound is another way to create a beautiful atmosphere in your home. Soothing music enhances your environment. Play music the next time you're cleaning, and see how motivated you'll be.

Make your house feel like a home. Surround yourself with beauty. Weekly, I buy fresh flowers to fill my colored vases around the house. This adds little touches of beauty.

The idea is to create a home you love. You should love the way it smells. You should love eating in your kitchen, or sharing with your family and friends in your family room.

You should love to sleep in your bedroom. Most people spend more time in their home than any other place. What you experience at home will mark you and your children for life. What mark are you making on your family? It's important that you take out the time to create a comfortable, beautiful home.

POINTS OF MOTIVATION

☞Buy Beautiful Towels: Bath sheets come as big as beach towels so you can wrap your whole body in comfort. Choose colors that are pleasing to your eye.

☞Buy Beautiful Dishes: Serve friends and family on pretty colorful dishes. Enhance your dining with pretty place settings. Don't wait for company to bring out the nice place settings.

☞Enhance Your Home with Fresh Flowers: Make it a ritual to buy fresh flowers when you grocery shop.

☞Beautify Your Home with Fragrances: Use scented candles for your rooms and scented sachets in your clothing drawers. Potpourri burners are a great way to add fragrance to a room, especially the kitchen.

☞Use file cabinets to file and organize bills and important papers.

My Motivational Journal

Who you are and, how you see the world has been influenced by your household when you were growing up. Describe the place you grew up.

How do you want your house to look now?

PART II
MENTAL
MOTIVATION

#10
Turn Off
the Television

*" TV is a language all it's own that destroys culture,
not add to it. TV is antiart - a reflection of consum-
erism that serves the power structure.
TV is about demographics."*
-Roseann Boss

Once I read an article that said your child may
be watching too much television because they
don't have any friends and are replacing relationships or social time with television viewing. Could this also be one of the reasons why
adults find themselves glued in front of the television? Viewing television has become the most
popular way to spend leisure time and has re-
placed meaningful relationship building. When
you watch too much television, you spend your
time watching other people do what they love
to do, when ironically it's probably the television

that is keeping you from doing what you love and are called to do. Everyday calculate, have I spent more time pursuing my purpose than I did watching television?

For the most part, television promotes a pessimistic attitude. People who watch excessive amounts of television read less, learn less, and run the risk of being depressed. If you want to stay motivated all the time, then limit your television viewing and carefully choose what programs you will watch. The Bible tells us in Proverbs, "As a man thinketh so is he." Remember that you ponder what you see.

That's why you have to be careful what you regularly view on television. For example, if you meditate on soap operas by watching them every day, your life will become like a soap opera. Every situation in life will seem dramatic and traumatic. All of the soaps are the same, someone is always cheating, dying, losing their mind, being kidnapped or depressed. Talk about living a defeated life! Meditate on that junk for a week and your motivation is out the window.

Violence, bad news and destruction have become commonplace in television entertainment. Most producers of programming say scenes of violent action accompanied with fear striking music, holds viewers attention to keep them from switching channels. The realistic and gory images displayed on the screens of American television have intensified. Local newscasts have increasingly focused on violence. Good news is rarely seen.

In essence, many producers are competing for ratings. If violence gets the ratings, whoever shows the most violence wins. Be aware that such violent programming can have negative effects on your attitude. Watching just one hour of this stuff can leave you feeling totally oppressed.

Unless I'm using my televsion time as a part of my scheduled recreation, I always try to do another task while the television is on. I only allow myself and my children to view a maximum of eight hours of television per week. I've found that if you schedule your television time, you'll be more selective about what you watch. You'll also tend to stay more focused on accomplishing your goals in life. The more you cut off the television, the more time you'll have to enjoy life. For one week, try using all your television time to work on a project you've been thinking about. Do something productive that will move you closer to accomplishing one of your desired goals. Did you know research shows that most non-readers are avid television watchers? Television is a real "no-brainer" activity. You don't have to use any brain-power to watch it. Opt for reading a good book instead of watching your favorite television show.

Recent research has found that watching excessive amounts of television can lead to obesity, because it encourages eating at the expense of exercise. Children watch an average of twenty-six hours of television per week and adults watch an average of twenty-one hours per week. That's a total of forty-seven hours you could use to develop yourself or your children to realize your dreams and goals.

I found a few inspiring quotes about television watching that may jar your thinking:

"Even if every program were educational and every advertisement bore the seal of approval of the American Dental Association, we would still have a critical problem. It's not just the programs, but the act of watching television hour after hour that's destructive."
-Ellen Goodman

"McLuhanism and the media have broken the back of the book business; they've freed people for the shame of not reading. They've rationalized becoming stupid and watching television."
-Pauline Kael

"No wonder Americans are discouraged about their life. TV watching is the number one leisure activity every day of the week."
-Stacia Pierce

POINTS OF MOTIVATION

☞For one week keep a television diary log. How many hours did you watch and what did you get out of the program?

☞List five things that you could do with your televsion time.

☞Monitor the programs your family views.

☞During the day, do chores as you watch television.

☞Go on a television fast for one full week and calculate all the extra time you have.

☞Play games instead of television viewing.

☞Make your children go outside and play instead of watching television.

MY MOTIVATIONAL JOURNAL

Why do you watch television?

Explain the nature of the shows you watch. What is drawing you to view these particular programs?

Do you watch any shows that you would be embarrassed to watch in front of those you respect? Explain.

#11
Prioritize &
Organize

"The purpose of order is to increase productivity and create comfort."
-Author Unknown

The phone rang. As I listened to the frustrated voice on the other end, I recognized it as one of the ladies from my women's leadership team. She began with, "I don't know how I'm going to make it," in a frazzled tone. "I can't seem to get my life in order, there's so much that I want to do, but there's never enough time to do it all." There was a long pause, then sobbing. I recognized this as the frustration of a young mother on the other end. I said, "Let's meet tomorrow after church."

The next day as I met with the young mother, my advice was, "You have to prioritize and

and organize your life." I went on to say, "The three keys you need to implement in your life are: to plan, pray and perform."

To Plan
Most people enter each day haphazardly assuming things will simply work themselves out and eventually they'll have more time. While this approach is very easy, it is also a very nonproductive approach. When you begin to plan, think, what are my ultimate goals in life? What dreams do I want to achieve? What do I really value most? Answering these questions will help you put your life in perspective as you minimize what you get involved in. Life is a lot easier when you have a plan.

Next, you must realize the season of your life. A new mother with small children has to focus on parenting, then address other pursuits. A few simple strategies will keep you focused and calm throughout your day. Planning your next day's activities can be rewarding. So, when the day is over, snuggle in bed with your Prayer & Purpose Planner, or notebook and create yourself a "To-do" list.

As you peacefully sit in bed, close your eyes and think of what you need to complete the next day. Include work schedules, children's activities, schoolwork, lunch, grocery shopping, meetings, special projects, classes, phone calls, your husband's needs, cleaning and appointments. Then write out your day's activities in order of importance. This simple gesture will add peace to your life.

Before I get into bed, I usually choose my outfit, iron it and hang it in my closet ready for the next morning. Knowing what you're wearing the next day saves you about fifteen to twenty minutes of morning preparation. You'll find that planning will cause you to go to bed feeling in control, and wake up feeling motivated. In the morning, review your plans. Don't start your day until you have it finished. Everyday is important and your success in life is determined by how well you plan out each day.

PRAY:
We have to learn to commit our plans to God in prayer. Communication with God is an essential component of getting and *staying* organized.

Pray daily for God's will to be done in your life. Ask the Lord to guide you in your decisions throughout the day. Seek God's wisdom on any additional plans He may have for you that you may have forgotten. Prayer doesn't have to be long and drawn out. Just communicate with God and yield to His will for your life.

PERFORM

To perform means: to fulfill, to execute an action or process. My personal definition of perform is, to follow through on what you have planned. Try to complete each item on your list, but if you don't complete it before the day ends, it's OK, at least you accomplished something. The feeling of accomplishment is very rewarding. Motivated people get things done.

If you don't know where your time is going, keep a diary for one week. Record how you spend every day. Record how you spend every twenty minutes. After one week, record what you did and what you want to change. Don't allow interuptions to stop you. If you're on a roll, don't stop everything when the phone rings, a neighbor stops by, or the mail comes.

POINTS OF MOTIVATION

☞Do the important things first. Tackle the day's main task before you take on the other less important ones.

☞Don't start a new task until you have everything, like supplies and the proper information to get the project underway.

☞Make time to organize.

☞Use a file cabinet and put all important papers, (bills, birth certificates, life insurance polices, social security cards, baptismal certificates etc.) in categorized file folders. Now, when you need an important paper, you don't waste precious time searching for information you already have.

☞Keep an appointment calendar. Use a coordinated system to keep track of projects. You don't want to be the kind of person who always forgets their doctor's appointment or their children's conferences.

☞ Set your clock five minutes ahead, so you can have extra time to get an important task done and stay on schedule.

☞ Learn to turn down requests that interfere with your priorities and goals.

☞ Solicit help where needed. Don't be afriad to use professional services, or ask a friend or family member to help with a task to free yourself up to be more effective.

☞ Shop during the hours that others don't.

☞ Put up a bulletin board. Post all important reminders like parent/teacher conferences and other family events.

☞ Keep up with your keys. Designate a hook or basket to always place your keys. Make it a habit not to put them anywhere else but in their designated spot.

☞ Toys: Buy a big plastic bin to store all your children's toys so they can clean up and put their things away after playtime.

☞Clothes: Only keep what you really love to wear, so you avoid having a closet full of too small, unused, outdated outfits.

My Motivational Journal

Are you devoting enough time to the things you really want and need to do?

Sketch out a picture of your perfect day if there were no limitations. Write down everything you would do from the time you get up in the morning, until the time you go to bed at night.

#12
Post Up an
Inspiring Photo

"Create an intense picture of where you are going."
-Dexter Yager

Visualizing yourself the way you desire to be is a classic way to motivate yourself towards a target. Many women who were at their ideal weight before gaining extra pounds have posted an inspiring photo from their past to encourage them to get back in shape. To stimulate myself to exercise and get back to my pre-pregnancy weight, I posted a photo of myself at my ideal weight in my Prayer and Purpose Planner.

If you are battling with a weight problem, try this technique: find a photo of yourself at your ideal weight or you can use a photo from a magazine and place yourself next to it. After doing this write out a confession of how you will look like the person in your inspirational photo.

I have designated places in the Prayer & Purpose Planner where you can paste what I call "Faith Photos." These pictures along with your written goals, prayer requests and scripture references, will give you a visual to reflect on daily while you are standing in faith and believing God for the manifestation of your prayer requests.

Before I began speaking at numerous women's events, I took women's conference ads from magazines and pasted my photograph as one of the keynote speakers. I would look at the ads frequently and speak faith filled words over each of them. In a short time doors began to open and I began to speak frequently at women's events. Many great speakers and pastors have done this and they have been rewarded with positive results.

Get a photo of yourself on a mock cover of *Good Housekeeping, Working Mother, Success* or any magazine that aligns itself with your purpose. You can usually find these mock magazine booths at amusement parks or a local activity center.

With color printers and scanners, you can make your own inspirational posters. If you are struggling with parenting, make yourself a mother of the year poster on your home computer, or use one at the nearest copying center. Add five positive statements of faith about yourself and describe why you deserve to be Mother of the Year. Then confess those faith-filled words over yourself daily.

Before I actually had my own magazine (W.O.R.D. magazine), I created mock magazine covers with the women on them who I desired to be featured in my magazine. Within a few years, not only did I have *W.O.R.D. magazine*, but many of the people that I wanted to feature, ended up on the actual covers.

Use photographs as a visual tool to encourage yourself to move toward your dreams. Glamour photos are wonderful for personal inspiration. During the photo shoot, you are treated like a movie star. You get the chance to wear a dazzling outfit, have your makeup done and look like royalty. The pictures come out magazine perfect. Glamour photos are a big boost to your self-esteem and a great source of motivation. Photographs have a magnetic pull in relation to your goals and dreams.

You've heard the phrase a picture is worth a thousand words. We'll it's true. When you see photos of yourself making great accomplishments, it increases your self-esteem and gives you proof of your victories. Get some pictures taken of yourself that you really like and begin pasting them up with your faith statements. Your life is worth making a visual documentation of your dreams, goals and accomplishments.

POINTS OF MOTIVATION

☞Make yourself a photo journal with pictures of you accomplishing great things in your past, then write how you felt and tell about the events.

☞Take photographs with people who are important to you; mentors, teacher, friends, family, famous people you meet and post them in your home office or den as a reminder of all the great people whom you have come in contact with.

☞Make yourself a magazine cover with your photograph on the cover and the feature story about you. Example: "Money mangagement tips from expert_____."
                                                          your name here

☞Make a motivational story book with your photos.

☞Make a photo calender with your pictures and a motivational quote under each photo. "I'm an achiever." "I'm more than a conquerer."

MY MOTIVATIONAL JOURNAL

What magazine cover would you like to be on? What would the heading say?

Do you run towards or from the camera when pictures are being taken and why?

#13
Browse
Through Your
Photo Album

*"To pick up a photo album and bask in the good
memories, is therapeutic."*
-Stacia Pierce

If you don't already have a photo album, then
begin one. You'll be more likely to reflect on
and share memories with friends and family
when your photos are put in an album. Don't
leave your photos around the house, stuffed in
the same packets they were in when they came
from the store.

I'm sure you have heard the saying, " A picture is worth a thousand words." It is so much
easier to explain a place, person or event with
photographs. Photos are proof. They give
your words validity. Sometimes a camera can
be a nuisance to carry along, but the value

of the photos far outweigh the inconvenience of carrying the camera. Today you can grab a disposable camera almost anywhere.

I remember one of my recent trips to a seminar. I didn't want to be bothered, so I didn't But at the seminar, I got the chance to meet a very well known best selling author and speaker. Oh, how I wished I'd brought my camera. I knew that the following morning would be my last chance to see and speak with this person before my departure. So I bought a disposable camera from the hotel gift shop and had a friend take a picture of me with the speaker. My whole family can enjoy the experience now.

Over the last four to five years, direct sales companies have started up that sell photo albums and supplies to decorate and dress them up. Some gift shops carry unique photo albums with accessories especially for children in sports, birthday party memories, vacations, etc. Adding special notes, designs, stickers and quotes to dress up your photos makes your photo album truly memorable and exciting to look at.

By investing a little time in your photo albums you can create a book of joyful memories to leave for your family's next generation. You might be thinking, "What should I take photos of?" Take photos of your children doing special things, their class and teachers, famous people, vacation sights, your mentors, family and holiday gatherings. To reflect back on these photographs will stir up joyful memories

Before I opened my former makeup boutique in the mall, I traveled to New York, Chicago and a few other metropolitan cities to view store layouts. I took a picture of a candy shop that caught my attention. It was the closest thing I'd seen that resembled the way I wanted to design and display my makeup products.

I took copies of pictures and posted them up on a story board and shared it with my staff. Because of the photographs, they couls see my vision and everyone was motivated to help me achieve the look I wanted. So many creative ideas were sparked, that when the store opened, women commented that they felt like a kid in a candy store. With the makeup being displayed in glass candy jars, it reminded the women of their childhood and enticed them to indulge.

Take inspiring photos to put into your album. Photos that will get you thinking creatively, photos that reflect ideas relating to your purpose in life. The next time you need a lift, pick up your photo album and bask in the good memories.

4 Ways to Take Star Photos

✮Determine the shape of your subject and hold your camera vertically or horizontally to accommodate it. Don't take a vertical shot of someone lying down for instance.

✮ Study the subject from all sides to choose the best angle to take your photo. Consider standing or sitting on a step, a chair, or on the floor.

★Imagine the picture as it will appear in a frame. Try to close in on the subject to exclude any surrounding distractions that don't belong.

★Film speed guidelines for 35mm cameras: 100ASA best for outdoors; 400 ASA for inside; and 200 ASA works well in either situation.

MOTIVATIONAL POINTS

☞**Create Photo Journals**
Tell stories about the photos by adding names, dates, titles and reflections.

▤**Friendship Journals-** Record dear moments you've spent in the company of your best friends.

▤**Vacation Journals-**Write out a list of things you want photos of on your next vacation and take along your photo journal to record daily activities and special moments. Leave a space to paste the photos once the film gets developed. Don't forget to collect stamps, tickets, menus, brochures, maps and other distinctive mementos to add to your travel journal.

▤**Success Journals-**Write about all the successes you had growing up and as an adult. Document things like, academic achievements, awards presented, contests you won, graduations, career advancements and paste inspiring photos that relate to these achievements.

☞Make a photo calendar with your most recent vacation photos.

☞Visit a craft or office supply store and pick up tools to help create inspiring photo albums.

☞Send some photos with a note to a friend.

☞ Use your computer: with the proper software, you can store and manipulate photographic images at home. With the help of a scanner, you can turn your photos into cards, calendars or e-mail to send to a friend.

☞Keep a scrapbook basket handy with all your tools in it, acid-free paper, pens, glue, tape, albums, sheet protectors, templates, patterned edged scissors, die cut frames, stickers, patterned rulers, stencils, doillies, and rubber stamps.

☞Keep photos in a colorful file folder separated and catagorized so while scrapbooking, you have exactly what you need.

MY MOTIVATIONAL JOURNAL

What story does your photo album tell about you?

What would you like to take photos of?

#14
Continue
to Grow

"We will be victorious if we have not forgotten how to learn."
- Rosa Luxemburg

Make it a personal goal to become a life long learner. You'll be much more interesting if you continue to grow. Most people make a decision to stop growing and learning once they get out of school. They possess the "I'm glad it's over" mentality.

Take a moment to review the knowledge you have acquired or mastered in your life this past year. How many courses or seminars have you attended since you graduated from high school? How many books have you read? Do you listen to audio tapes weekly?

When I speak at women's conferences, I often take a survey or ask the ladies to write and tell me which particular principles I shared with them totally transformed their life. The most recurring response was, that once they followed my advice to read, listen to educational audio cassettes, go to seminars and women's conferences and upgrade their skills, their lives took on greater meaning.

What's the last book you've read that challenged you to improve your life? The next time you choose a book to read, choose it with the intention to grow. Did you know you can become an expert in the field of your choice by reading twenty minutes every day for six months on a specific subject?

Sometimes you can get de-motivated by reflecting on your learning regrets from your past. Do you have any regrets, "if only's" or "what if's?" You can change all of that. Don't let the past stifle you. What do you want to learn? When was the last time you visited your local library? Everything you want to learn can probably be found there, but you must look.

Over the last ten years, I decided to build my home library of books, audio and video materials to contribute to my personal growth. Now I have access to information that can help me achieve my purpose. By building your own personal library, you will have a reservoir of information at your fingertips.

What you learn internally will never be in vain. God has an awesome way of using a prepared person. You never know when you'll need to draw on your personal information bank to give a speech, conduct a meeting, counsel a friend, start a business, lead a bible study or write an agenda. To stay excited about life, you must have a desire to learn.

Direct your learning process in areas concerning your purpose. The best way to do this is to start with five to seven main categories that relate to what interests you and what you are called to do.

Over the last ten years I have strategically chosen what main subjects I wanted to learn about,

For example, my mission in life is to motivate ordinary women to live extraordinary lives; which is the title of my new book project about achieving purpose.

I created a learning system called The Purpose Files©. It is one that myself and many women I have taught used to transform our lives. The Purpose Files© is an organized file system for information you gather which is related to your purpose. This system has been used in one form of the another, over the years by some of the most successful people in our society. The actual technique varies I believe, based on the different personality types.

I motivate women by teaching information in the areas of personal growth, health and nutrition, image enhancement, parenting/child development, leadership development, communication skills and spiritual growth. Those subjects make up my purpose files.

As a motivational speaker, I desire to stay current, so I'm always reading and researching to find new information to add to my files. The information I find also helps me when conversing with women. It gives me something substantial to discuss. Stimulate your mind with new information, it will keep you from becoming stale and predictable. Start a filing system of information related to your purpose.

If you have young children like I do, or if circumstances keep you from reading or learning as much as you like, you have to create a balance. Start by scheduling some personal growth time in your week, even if that means getting a sitter for a few hours so you can grow. Seize every opportunity to sneak in some personal growth time. Keep a book with you at all times, so if you are delayed, you can read.

To stimulate the women at our church to grow, I started a women's reading club. Every other month, I release a newsletter with three suggested books to read. At the end of our bible study classes, we do our book review. The response has been overwhelming. The women tell me they get so many ideas from the review.

It also keeps them highly motivated to read when they know there will be an opportunity to discuss the book. Joining a Christian reading club can be an excellent way to feed your mind.

Henry Ford said, "Anyone who stops learning is old whether at twenty or eighty." In contrast, anyone who keeps learning stays young. One of the greatest things in life is to keep your mind young. Research shows us that people who stop learning are more susceptible to Alzheimer's disease. If you have been feeling a little stale lately, maybe it's time to get going and get growing.

I suggest that you create a personal learning program for yourself which includes reading, listening to audio cassettes, attending seminars and conferences. Then watch how God will use you - a prepared person.

POINTS OF MOTIVATION

☞ Expand your knowledge.

☞ Enroll in a class at your local community college.

☞ Look up a word per week in your dictionary. Practice using it in sentences to expand your vocabulary.

☞ Play word games with your family and friends like, Scrabble™, or Mad Gab™, it will stimulate the entire family.

☞ Listen to educational tapes while driving to work or doing housework. Take the time you would have used for mundane activities and use it as growth time.

☞ Check out videos from the library on a subject you've always wanted to learn more about.

☞Write down facts or interesting quotes you want to remember in a personal growth journal and then categorize your information for future reference.

☞Find a more experienced person to learn from and adopt them in your life as a mentor.

☞Attend at least two educational or informative conferences each year.

☞Education helps us to live a higher quality life by continually stretching our minds. Don't ever decide you've learned enough.

How Are you Growing Quiz

1. Name two magazines that you subscribe to.

2. Name a book and author on the New York Times best sellers list this year.

3. Give the name of a popular Broadway show.

4. What's the popular story now in World News.

5. Who is Madeline Albright?

6. Name the last state you visited this year outside of your own.

7. What is that state's most popular attraction?

No matter how you answered, you still need to continue to grow. However, if you were unable to answer two or more, you will want to put your personal growth plan in action immediately.

MY MOTIVATIONAL JOURNAL

Can you get excited about learning?
Explain.

Write a list of the first five things you will do
to begin your personal growth program.

#15
Read

"Just the knowledge that a good book is awaiting one at the end of a long day make that day happier."
-Kathleen Norris

Reading is fundamental. It will help keep you stay alert to life. I get so excited when I read a truly good book that challenges me to change, or motivates me to keep moving forward. I also enjoy the books that just brighten your day or take you on an adventure to places you have never been before.

Ever since I was a child, I indulged in the joy of reading. Yet it wasn't until I became an adult and got serious about my purpose in life that I began to read voraciously. Books have not only helped to mold and shape me into becoming a better person, but the books I read ignited my gifts and talents that were lying dormant. I remember reading a particular book that showed me clear directions of where I should be headed in life.

Books are a powerful tool, they have the ability to expand your vision. They can give you strategies to overcome difficult situations. Some of the most profound ideas have come to people as a result of reading a book. Many of my best ministry topics have come to me while reading. I can recall reading a children's book about women in the bible it gave me ideas which compelled me to use great women from the bible as examples for my one of my very popular conference messages, "Attitudes of Achievers."

Learning new things makes life exciting. Reading allows people to expand their awareness and learn the knowledge necessary to obtain the skills to fulfill their specific purpose. I often run into women who are in leadership positions, yet they tell me that they barely read. No wonder we have so many leaders who have low-self esteem, and must rely on the skills of others to be effective.

You must make time to read useful books, magazines, and periodicals. The most important skill to acquire is learning how to learn. A fun way to accomplish this is by reading or listening to audio tapes.

"Everyone who rises above common level has received two educations: the first from teachers and the second: more personal and important from yourself."
- Edward Gibbon

Books are the basis of literature, composition, history, world events, vocabulary and everything else. When I'm reading books I underline new words I haven't heard and look up the definitions. Learning new words expands my vocabulary. Learn just one new word every day, in five years you can talk with anybody about almost anything.

Research was done at Georgetown Medical

school that showed when one's vocabulary increase, in 100% of the cases with no exception, their I.Q. automatically increases. Read something informative or inspirational every day. Reading for twenty minutes at just 240 words a minute will enable you to read twenty 200 page books each year. That's eighteen more than the average person reads. You will gain an enormous, competitive advantage.

"As you grow ready for it, somewhere or other you will find what is needful for you in a book."
- George MacDonald

Keep a basket of books by your bed. Save twenty to thirty minutes before you go to sleep to read. I use gold baskets full of books as decoration in my bedroom.

Read for purpose. What categories are you interested in? Focus on the subjects that are related to your purpose in life. Begin to buy books on those related subjects. The pleasure of all reading is doubled when one reads a book that answers questions related to their life.

Maintain a balance between Christian reading material and secular books. Don't be religious and think that you can only read Christian books. Just carefully select your books, so that you are not feeding your mind philosophies that are contrary to your Christian beliefs and the word of God. Note that many secular books provide needful information for your purpose in life.

The Bible is the best motivational publication in print. It contains the answers to all of life's problems. Schedule regular bible reading time. Try reading from all different versions of the bible. The standard is *King James*, but some of the other translations broaden your understanding like the *Amplified, New King James, The True Living Bible* or one of my personal favorites, *The Message Bible.*

I recently attended a seminar where Barbara Bush, the former first lady, spoke. Her speech was about attacking the problem of becoming a more literate America. Mrs. Bush shared many heart-touching stories of how illiteracy has hindered and is affecting our youth. Her speech compelled me to take a more active role in getting people to read more, particularly women.

Children growing up in homes where reading is valued are more likely to be good readers. Approximately 80 million people in the United States are illiterate or have poor reading skills. They did not learn to read in school, so now they settle for less in their relationships, and careers. What's even sadder is, people who know how to read, yet choose not to. It's been proven that the most fulfilled people love to read, listen to educational and motivational cassettes, go to seminars and upgrade their skills daily.

I began the book reading club for the women at my church to help them get more motivated about reading. The club was an instant success. The women who participate enjoy reading now, especially since they have the opportunity to share and discuss with others what they've read.

When mothers read, it helps the whole family. It helps them have more interesting conversation with their husbands and children.

Reading creates a reserve bank. It gives you more information than you would normally use right away, but the knowledge is always there for you to draw upon. Do a book report on every book you read to record and highlight the most important facts. Don't ever forget that God will never waste a prepared person. Be ready to fulfill God's exciting plan for your life.

POINTS OF MOTIVATION

☞Subscribe to at least one magazine so that you can stay current.

☞Always read with a pen, paper and highlighter in hand.

☞Try reading at least one book a month.

☞Set goals to increase the amount of books you read.

☞Read material that will enhance what you're called to do.

☞Reading is a productive and restorative way to spend some time alone. It can be very re-laxing and a good mini-escape.

☞Keep a reading log/journal or do book re-ports. It will increase your reading effective-ness. I made book report forms that cause you to think about what the book meant to you and what you will do with the information.

☞Reading exposes you to new worlds of people and ideas. Books will open you up to new topics and points of view. Your philosophy of life will be shallow if you do not read.

☞It isn't always easy to learn. Choose books that challenge you intellectually. Don't always opt for the easy reads. Buy a book that is longer that you normally would read. Choose a book that has words you may have to look up. Come out of your reading comfort zone.

MY MOTIVATIONAL JOURNAL

How many books have you read in the last year?
A. What was the content of these books?
B. How did they help you to grow?

What subject would you like to become an expert in?

#16
Listen to
Positive Audio
Tapes

"The most fulfilled people love to read, listen to positive educational audio tapes, go to seminars and upgrade their skills daily."
-Stacia Pierce

The commuting time you have in your car is an excellent time for self-education. Research at the University of California reveals, if you live in a metropolitan area and drive 12,000 miles each year you can acquire the equivalent of two years worth of a college education while driving. When you get into your car, listen to informative motivational tapes and you will arrive at your destination better informed and inspired to do more with your life.

I often start off my day by listening to positive audio tapes in my car and then end my day the same way. As a result, I am able to keep my brain alert and the information I take in keeps me excited.

Positive cassettes can directly affect your self-esteem. The more positive messages you hear, the better equipped you become to live a more productive life, which results in a high level of self-esteem.

While attending a seminar, I was listening to a speaker talk about how listening to positive audio tapes will not only increase your education level, but will help you achieve more. The information wasn't new to me, in fact I had taught the same principles for years, but for some reason it triggered something in me as if a light bulb had come on!

Immediately, I began to think about my daughter Ariana who was seven at the time and what an advantage she would have, if she started now listening to positive audio tapes on a regular basis. So I purchased a few sets of

Christian motivational messages for children, for her to listen to. I didn't see the impact it had on her life immediately, but several months later, she referred to one of the points the speaker made on her tapes. In reference to it, Ariana decided to make some positive changes in her life, for example, to give more. I now know that no matter what your age, the impact of positive audio tapes is life changing.

At church we minister a very positive, life changing message on a weekly basis and encourage the congregation to purchase the audio tapes to replay the messages. Most of the time hearing a message once isn't good enough. It's through repetition that a message sinks in and you adapt to the new information, then you begin to apply it.

Get into the habit of purchasing tapes when you hear a good message that speaks into your current situation, or gives information that can be beneficial to your future. Build yourself an audio cassette library. Value your tapes, put them back into their jackets so they don't get lost. Buy a book case or stacking crates to organize your library. When my husband and I hear a good speaker, we tend to buy several of their tape messages, if not every thing they have. We have learned the value of, getting all the information you can from a good speaker. In our library, our audio tapes are categorized by speakers. We may have as many as twenty tape series by one speaker.

Be sure you know what you are listening to. Everything that seems positive isn't good for you. For the most part, listening to positive Christian tapes are the safest way to go. That doesn't mean every speaker or minister that is Christian is automatically positive. I've heard some pretty depressing Christian speakers before, and I chose to stay clear of their material because it wasn't edifying.

Use a little discernment when choosing positive audio tapes to listen to. Remember, what you meditate on, you will eventually become.

Listening to positive audio tapes has saved lives. If you are sick, you can increase your faith for healing by listening to positive healing messages that are based on the word of God. Nasir Sidikki, tells the testimony of his wife. At twenty-five years of age, her hands and legs were twisted, when she was five months pregnant she collapsed. She had no feeling in her body from the neck down. Mrs. Sidikki then became blind and paralyzed. Doctors put eight needles in her head and diagnosed her condition as multiple sclerosis (of which there is no cure).

After two years of consistently (twenty-four hours a day) listening to faith filled teaching tapes on healing, around the clock (she couldn't open her Bible), she became totally healed, (and it's documented). Mrs. Sadikki went on to attend and graduate from Rhema Bible Training Center with a 4.0 grade point average. She now ministers around the country, giving her testimony and helping to save the lives of others.

Listening to positive audio cassettes have helped to change peoples economic status. I have heard many testimonies of wealthy people who state that when they began a self-improvement program which included listening to positive audio tapes, their economic status improved.

Peter Daniels came from a broken home, failed in every grade of school and was a third generation welfare recipient. In 1959 he attended a Billy Graham crusade and accepted Christ as his Lord and Savior.

Rejected as a missionary due to his lack of education, he began a self- improvement program of listening to positive audio tapes and reading. This resulted in his becoming a millionaire land developer and one of Australia's top motivational speakers. Using biblical principles, Mr. Daniels lectures on real estate, leadership management and goal setting.[1]

It has been said that if you listen to tapes on any one subject for only one hour a day five days a week, in five years you will end up with the equivalent of a Ph. D in that subject. You may not need a Ph. D in your area, but the point is you can use listening to positive audio tapes as a way to increase your knowledge.

When can you find the time for tapes?

* While in your car or traveling by plane.

* While in the tub or showering.

* While you're going to sleep at night.

* While you are cleaning the house.

* While exercising.

POINTS OF MOTIVATION

☞Listen to reports or audio tapes of people who have overcome similar circumstances to your own.

☞Purchase a portable cassette player with an adapter so you can to listen to your tapes any-where, anytime.

☞The most important accessory you could ever put in your car is a cassette player. It has the ability to change your life.

☞Listen to Bible teachings on audio cassette on a regular basis.

☞Purchase a Walkman so you can listen to tapes while traveling, exercising or cleaning the house.

☞If you have to give a speech or conduct a meeting, spend an hour beforehand listening to positve audio tapes. Your presentation will be more lively.

☞If you are going through a rough time in your life, allow positive audio tapes to play all night long while you are sleeping. The positive words will encourage your inner man while you rest.

MY MOTIVATIONAL JOURNAL

What was the last positive audio tape you heard?
What was it about? How did it affect your life?

Lord, I need to listen to positive audio tapes on the
subject of _____ so I can
_____

#17
Attend Women's Events

"Fill your life with new experience. Not only will you live a more quality life, but it's the only way to grow."
-Stacia Pierce

Conferences, seminars, workshops, bible studies and other meetings geared specifically toward women will usually address issues that cover a broad spectrum of women. These meetings are usually very motivational and informative.

A good women's meeting will offer you the opportunity to laugh and learn. If you're like most women today, then you are faced with many demands. You need information, encouragement and support. Becoming a part of a good women's bible study will help you develop your spiritual life, while getting practical answers to life's everyday questions.

I teach a Bible study called " Women In the Word" which meets twice a month. My bible study agenda has five parts: a time for fellowship so women can build relationships; a brief time for praise and worship, so we can get our minds focused on the Lord; a time in the Word, where an inspirational message is given with practical instructions for daily living; and a time for personal ministry, where the women's leadership team will take prayer requests. I conclude with praise reports so women are strengthened in their Christian walk. Most church founded bible studies operate in a similar format, so you can get very good ministry by attending one.

Every year you should plan to attend at least one women's conference. Most conferences are life changing. A lot of preparation goes into a good conference to make sure that you are ministered to. I host a big three day annual women's conference each May and we begin planning for it the year before. We plan all the details of the conference. In January through May, we pray for the success of the conference and for all the women who will attend.

There's a different experience you get from a small women's group, than you get from a conference. A small group offers the opportunity to develop friendships, continued spiritual growth and encouragement.

A conference on the other hand, lays a foundation by offering sound teaching on principles. These principles should compel you to make changes in your life and inspire you to build upon what you have learned.

The word conference means confer. It's a meeting for discussion. So you get the opportunity to come together with several other women from a variety of backgrounds and locations and you confer. You consult with other women about the messages you heard.

I can remember years ago flying several hundred miles to attend a three day women's conference. I was excited about the time away and how I thought it would be refreshing. It was awesome, life changing and truly inspiring. I received much more than I bargained for.

I met several very interesting, and talented women who are still a part of my life today. We ate lunch together and shared how we would implement all of the good advice we received. The messages were a real boost to my spiritual life. I took detailed notes and set goals to use the information I learned. The materials I purchased helped to shape my ministry into what it is today.

It's important that when you attend women's conferences you plan to buy several books and tapes. I always take what I call, " seed money" to a women's conference. Even if you purchased a ticket, the event is probably worth three times your ticket price. Plan to give at offering time. Remember, what you sow into others you will reap.

Feed me Lord
Let me drink of the Living water
Fill me up
Till I overflo
Feed me Lord
with the pour of Your Spirit
In Your Word
I must Surely grow.

How Do You Find A Good Women's Conference?

If your church doesn't host one annually, then subscribe to popular Christian magazines. This is an avenue to find out what is taking place. Call your favorite ministries and ask if they plan to have a women's conference anytime during the year. Get on the mailing list of your favorite ministries. Ask friends in other states if their church is hosting a conference. Your friends may know about a women's conference but, just have never gotten around to sharing the information with you.

How to Get the Most Out of a Conference:

1. Prepare in advance: Pray and ask the Lord to lead you to meet the right people. Pray that your experience will be life changing.

2. Be optimistic: Believe that it's going to be good.

3. Show interest in new people: be friendly, talk to new people, exchange phone numbers and addresses. Maintain a caring attitude toward the people you meet.

4. **Take notes:** Take your planner, pens, highlighter and Bible. Take notes from the speakers' messages and write down ideas or comments as they come to you.

5. **Buy the conference tapes:** You'll never remember everything. Buy all the tapes so you can replay this glorious occasion. You can also share the tapes with friends who couldn't make it. Usually, they are discounted if you buy them before you leave.

6. **Sow Seed:** Give in the offering. That shows your support of the meeting.

7. **Go to all of the sessions:** Many times there will be day workshops along with the night sessions. Don't skip the day workshops, that's probably where you'll get most of your information.

8. **Buy the speakers books and tapes:** How exciting it is to take home some goodies to follow-up on what you've learned. I usually begin looking at my material in the hotel room.

9. Maximize the Impact: Get mementos - a brochure, workbook, picture, if possible, an autograph book. Be thankful: Send a note of appreciation to the host.

10. Make a Journal Entry. If the conference lasts more than one day, review your notes, and make a journal entry of how the messages have affected your life before you retire at night.

POINTS OF MOTIVATION

☞Always dress confidently when attending a conference, otherwise you will shy away from meeting people.

☞Take all your learning tools: Bible, pens, paper, calendar and a Walkman.

☞Take all of your networking tools: planner, address cards (if you are in business for yourself) business information and address book to record new names and numbers.

☞Smile. More people will approach you, and you'll make some really important contacts.

☞Read over all of your conference materials thoroughly, they will probably give you all the times locations and plans about every event taking place during the conference.

☞Book your hotel rooms early, don't wait until right before the registration deadline, or you'll probably be without a room or end up paying more than the discounted price.

MY MOTIVATIONAL JOURNAL

I will try to find a women's conference this year that addresses the issues I need help with in my life, which are:

At the next women's conference I attend, I will meet three new people and share with them four positive things about myself, which are:

#18
Design a
Quality Life-style

"How we spend our days is of course how we spend our lives, there is no shortage of good days. It is good lives that are hard to come by."
-Anne Dillard

Life-style is culture - the appreciation of art, the performing arts, good music, museums, sculptures, literature, symphonies and plays. It includes a taste for the fine, the unique and the beautiful.

Five years ago my husband and I decided to live quality life-style. It took the renewing of our minds to achieve our goal. We had to stop measuring everything by the amount of it's cost, but rather by the value it holds.

Our first Broadway play we attended in Manhattan, New York, was "Annie." The tickets were one hundred dollars each! We had excellent second row seats. Our first thoughts questioned whether or not little Annie was really worth it, but we resisted the urge to remain average and went for it. The experience of seeing "Annie" was life changing. It opened us up to a whole new arena of enjoyment. Since then we have been to several Broadway shows and musicals with our entire family as well as our friends.

To design a life worth living, it may cost you more. But it's worth it to save up to buy something special, and of lasting value like theater tickets, a piece of art, a special pen, or quality clothes. You may have to create a "life-styles fund" and put money into it on a consistent basis so you can enjoy the finer things in life.

Having a quality life-style is rewarding excellence whenever you find it. For instance, I go to my hairdresser every week and she has an assistant who washes your hair before you see the stylist. The young lady who washes my hair does such a superb job. She massages my scalp and deep conditions my hair. The experience is totally therapeutic. I reward her stand out service with a tip. She is always very grateful. It motivates me to see her appreciation.

Quality living demands that you not take the small things in life for granted. Reward people for going out of their way. Don't exclude your mate or children. The next time you receive exceptional service, give a good tip.

To give your life some panache, not only will you have to reward excellence, but you must *practice personal excellence*. Vince Lombardi put it this way; "The quality of a person's life is in direct proportion to their commitment to excellence."

Recently, I taught a group of women about the art of letter writing, and how it adds to the quality of their life. Sadly, letter writing has nearly become a lost art in our modern, fast-paced world. The gift of a handwritten letter brings exceptional joy to both the writer and the receiver. A short, timely, letter can enhance someone's day. You'll be sure to receive some great letters in return. Letters mingle the soul, so it's one of the best ways to build intimacy into a friendship.

Every month I pick a day for my daughter and I to write letters and cards to our friends and relatives. We enthusiastically talk about how our receivers will probably respond. To make the letter writing fun, have your tools handy and attractively arranged where you can see them. Collect cards, stationery and stamps that express your personality. I keep my tools in the kitchen in pretty, colorful and decorative storage boxes.

Travel the world to expand your knowledge about life. Your perspective is enlightened when you travel. You discover life's treasures, meet interesting people, and develop some unique relationships.

The experiences brought about by my travels have positively affected my life. Visiting Manhattan caused me to think big. California inspired a life long interest in health and nutrition. Learning about the history of Chicago expanded my mind. Disney World in Orlando, Florida, gave me a greater appreciation for our ability to visualize, dream, take action and then watch those things become a reality. I've traveled to many other places and each time I see a new part of the world, my life is enhanced and I become a more interesting person.

Plan to do some traveling, even if it's only driving distance. The next time you travel, look for life's treasures. Your experience will be more rewarding. Take photos. As you already know, a picture is worth a thousand words. You can use these visual words to share the essence of your life with generations to come.

Don't settle for a second rate life. Every woman can work within her means to design a quality life she and her family can be proud of. When you deprive yourself of a quality life you rob yourself of the happiness that can be easily achieved. Begin now to invest richness in the things you do on a regular basis. As you add some style to your life you'll be motivated to live and share with others a life you enjoy.

MOTIVATIONAL POINTS

☞Visit a stationery store and discover what paper appeals to you. What themes, colors and textures do you like the most?

☞Get a subscription to *Conde` Nast Traveler* magazine and take an exotic vacation right from your living room.

☞Go look at fine writing pens in a jewelry store or stationery shop. Choose a style and fit for yourself. Use it to sign documents and write your letters.

☞Buy yourself and a friend theater tickets to see a Broadway production. Afterwards, discuss your experience over a light dessert.

☞Plan a vacation and use this time. Look for little treasures to add to your life.

☞Go to a museum of interest

☞ Write thank you notes immediately! Keep cards on hand so you won't make the excuse that you don't have time.

☞ Tip your hairdresser, nail technician, gas station attendant, car washer, or yard maintenance person the next time they provide exceptional service for you.

☞ Write a letter to a friend you haven't talked to in a while. Tell them what's exciting in your life. Ask them to respond in writing by telling you what's exciting in their life.

MY MOTIVATIONAL JOURNAL

What experiences do you want to add to your life to make it more exciting? Make a list.

PART III

SPIRITUAL MOTIVATION

#19
Pray

"When you pray, you get into the stream of God's power. All you have to do is yield yourself to God... and you'll soon find yourself lifted above all obstacles, all storms, all difficulties."
-Kathryn Kuhlman

If a woman doesn't take time to replenish her relationship with the Lord and allow Him to fill her heart and mind it will eventually be noticeable in her attitude. Scripture tells us that out of the overflow of the heart, the mouth speaks. Our attitudes will reflect what we've stored in our hearts.

To replenish that all important relationship with our Heavenly Father, it is important to have the proper tools, plus a comfortable, familiar place to meet with God.

The familiarity draws you there, the tools gives

you confidence that you're on the right track, and the attractiveness will make you want to linger.

Silence is the most important sound for drawing near to God and meditating on His word. With two small children, I have to get up early before my family, to have my quiet time with the Lord. I don't bog myself down with time restraints; the point is to communicate with God daily.

My special place to meet with God is my bedroom. Some days, I gaze out the window while I sit on my white wicker prayer chair. Bright colors motivate me, so my room is decorated in yellow, fuschia and emerald green. As I quiet my mind to meditate on the things of God, I smile because my surroundings are so beautiful.

Next to my chair is my white wicker tool basket. It is filled with a few different bible translations, my Prayer and Purpose planner, my Bible study journal, a few devotionals, pens and highlighters.

The most motivating part of my prayer time is using my Prayer and Purpose planner. It's filled with photos of my family and friends for whom I'm praying. I keep photos of things related to my purpose with scriptural references or confessions next to them and phrases by each photo that specifies my request. Also listed there are ideas requring further direction from God before pursuing, and my dreams and goals for the future.

"The reason you don't have what you want, is that you don't ask God for it."
James 4:2 (TLB)

In my Prayer and Purpose planner, I also write answers to my prayers. In my prayer workshops I always tell women to commit their dreams and ideas to God through prayer. The reason you don't have what you want is that you don't ask God for it. Once God gets involved in your purpose and plans, He gives you direction and makes a way for divine connections and open doors to cause your desires to come to pass.

171

Use your prayer time as meditaion time. Daily, I meditate on the promises of God in His word. Then, after reviewing my Prayer and Purpose planner, and looking over all my faith photos, I close my eyes and envision the end result. I then think about how throughly applying the scriptures, God will cause the dreams in my life to come to pass. Prayer can literally change your life, it will take you from living a mundane, ordinary life to living an exciting, above average, extraordinary life.

Find a location, a special spot you can set aside as your prayer spot. Prayer is not a substitute for time in the Word, it will lead you to the Word. What prayer does is, allow God's presence into all areas of your life. You need God in all areas of your life to stay motivated.

POINTS OF MOTIVATION

☞Gather prayer tools- Bibles, devotionals, a Prayer and Purpose Planner or a notebook, pens, and highlighters. Often you will want to record what God is speaking to you and ideas that emerge from your prayer time.

☞Prayer has to be a life-style, not just something we do. Prayer should be done all day long. Communicate with God throughout the day, as things arise, say a quick prayer.

What the Bible says about prayer:
☞James 5:16 - "The effectual fervent prayer of a righteous man availeth much." Your prayers will avail when you are in right standing with God.

☞Matthew 21:22 - "And whatsoever things you ask in prayer, believe you will receive." Believe that God wants to give you things. Don't think it's wrong to ask God for things in your prayer time.

☞Pray about everything. Trials, finances, family relations, goals and dreams, a new car, protection, a new home, friendships, vacations, emotional hurts and your daily activities.

☞Pray over every new project you take on. You need to get used to spirit filled living; allowing God into all your endeavors.

☞Pray for favor on your job, with your boss and with people you desire to meet.

☞Pray with and for your friends who may be experiencing some trials.

☞Create a prayer list of needs you have and find scripture references to validate your requets.

☞Take a few hours to write out your prayers. These will become your daily confessions.

My Motivational Journal

Do you have a prayer place? Where is it? If you don't, find a spot in your home this week.

Are you committed to a daily time of prayer? If not, commit to a specific prayer. It doesn't have to be long, but it should be consistent.

#20
Study the Bible

*"I never saw a useful Christian who was not a
student of the Bible."*
- D. L. Moody

Bible study is different from reading. When
you study your bible, you are doing it for a
purpose, it's not just casual reading. Three
things should happen in bible study. It should,
(1.) instruct you to live a life that God approves
of, (2.) cause the results of the Word to be evi-
dent in your life, (this means that your life is
noticeable and exciting.) and (3.) give proper
understanding of the intent of the scriptures.

When studying your Bible, you receive such
awesome insight into the things of God and how
He operates. You'll discover from the Bible
that God has such a rewarding life planned for
you. It is God's desire for you to be an over-
comer and to succeed. He has provided His
word and His spirit to do so.

177

I take certain scriptures that are promised from God to me and write them down in my Prayer and Purpose Planner to confess them over myself.

Once I did a bible study in the book of Proverbs and it motivated me to make changes in my life. The book of Proverbs is full of wisdom and instruction for how to have a successful life.

You will know your bible study has been effective when you get answers to personal issues in your life. Effective bible study will cause negative situations in your life to change. Bible study is so motivating because your Christian walk will get stronger. Eventually, what you read becomes a part of who you are and what you believe. God is usually speaking to us about prevailing issues in our lives, so those issues will be what stands out to you as you study the bible. When you are tempted to sin, the scriptures you've studied will ring in your spirit (conscious).

The more you study, the more sensitive you will become to the voice of God. Once you gain an understanding of the scriptures it will give you greater discernment about people, situations and life in general. You'll be able to help others by using the scriptures. Bible study makes you a good counselor for your family friends and mentorees. Once you've experienced the Word, you will know what scriptures to use to help someone out of the situations they are in. You will be more convincing due to your personal experience in using the Word and having it work for you.

The following are common bible study questions with suggested answers and tips

Q. How do I fit bible study into my life?

A. The first thing you must do is change your attitude about bible study. Bible study should be approached as something that you enjoy rather than a chore or an interruption. Psalms 119:47 says; "And I will delight myself in thy commandments which I have loved." Once you get a love for the things of God and for living your life according to His word, then you will prioritize your time to fit bible study in. When you value something you make room for it.

Schedule your time for bible study. Write in your Planner what days and time you will set aside for study. Depending on your situation, whether you have small children , are single, or if your children are grown, will determine how often and how many days you can actually study your bible. My schedule changed with my last child, Ryan. I went from studying three days a week for two hours each day, to one day a week for about two hours.

Q. Where is the best place for me to study my bible?

A. A quiet place, free of distractions. Trying to study where people are around will prevent you from concentrating on the Word and hearing God's voice clearly. Quietness allows you to meditate on what you've studied, while you receive direction and motivation from God. Through quiet meditation, you can draw strength from the word of God to face situations throughout the day.

Have a private place where you can write notes. Designate a place where your study notes will stay intact and the information you've gathered won't get displaced. I suggest you get a notebook or journal just for bible study, then you will have a place where your personal improvement notes can remain private.

A comfortable place is important to the effectiveness of your bible study. You want a place where you can write and position your body properly. Don't lay down if you know that you'll fall asleep. Don't sit in a way that will give you neck cramps, stiffness, or headaches. For best results, try to have a moderate room temperature and proper lighting.

Q. What version of the Bible should I use to study?

A. The best bible version for you to study is the version that is easiest for you to understand. The version you choose will depend on your experience and familiarity with the bible. Different versions may be more appropriate for certain studies. Try to give yourself as many options as possible. When I first began to study the bible with my children, I used a Children's Bible. It's amazing the insight I get from reading it.

Most of the time I use the *King James*, the *Amplified* and the *New International* versions. I like the *Amplified* version for clarification, especially when I'm studying to prepare for a message. The *Amplified* is good for getting the most accurate understanding of the original manuscript. The *Amplified* also gives you a better understanding of the context and intent of the writer. It's a great version to give you other words and phrases that relate to the scriptures you are studying.

Also good for study is the *Thompson Chain Reference* Bible. It tracks a particular word or theme throughout the scriptures from Genesis to Revelation.

An *Annotated Bible* gives you columns of explanation of the scriptures. I wouldn't suggest this for beginning bible students, but as you grow in your studies you may deem it necessary. Remember, if you choose to use these versions, annotations are often the translator's opinion and may not be consistent with the intent of the scriptures. Personally, I rarely use one of these versions. My husband on the other hand, enjoys using it in his studies.

Q. Should I use certain tools to aid in my study?

A. Yes, to make your bible study more effective, you will need some tools such as the following:

📖 **An Exhaustive Concordance** to look up and learn the meaning of words.

📖**A Notebook, pen and highlighters** to highlight the scriptures that are important to you.

📖 **A Bible Dictionary** to get the biblical definitions

In my Bible I like to categorize my scriptures once I highlight them. I put a reference note as to what I use the scripture for. Many study helps are available. You may need to spend some time at the Christian bookstore in order to determine which study tools and brands will be most effective for you. You also have the option of getting bible study guides on a particular subject or a particular book of the Bible.

Q. Is there a certain way I should study?

A. The following are several different bible study methods you can use:

📖 **Word study-** Taking a particular word, finding it's meaning and context throughout the scriptures.

📖 **Lesson study-** Taking a particular lesson such as, "How To Be Disciplined" and finding the scriptures that show you how. This is my favorite and most frequently used method of study.

📖 **Book, Chapter and theme study-** Taking a book of the Bible and studying each chapter including the author, audience, culture, time in history and theme throughout, etc. For this type of study you may want to use a bible dictionary, bible reference book or a Customs and Manners book.

When you take out time to study God's word, you will develop an overcomers' image of yourself. Take the Bible and begin developing a scriptural success image of yourself. Start your study program today, your motivation and the outcome of your life depends on it!

POINTS OF MOTIVATION

☞ *"God's spirit and His word can change our lives into women of grace and wisdom."*
Sharon Daughtery

☞ *"God is looking for women who dare to believe His word!"*
-Mary Jean Pidgeon

☞ *"The Word is not just paper and ink...It's life"*
-Pat Harrison

☞ *"You must continually put the Word in your mind to keep it in agreement and at peace in your spirit."*
-Pat Harrison

☞ *"Give God's word first place in your heart because it is life and health to your body."*
-Dodie Osteen

☞ *"Take time to get away from the world and study God's word. Meditate on it and let it change you from the inside out."*
-Gloria Copeland

☞ *"Hours of prayer and study is of no effect if you do not enforce what is learned."*
-Cathy Duplantis

MY MOTIVATIONAL JOURNAL

Outline what type of bible study format you will commit to.

List five reasons why personal bible study is important to you getting the most accurate understanding of God's word.

#21
Take Some
Personal Time

*"Friendship with oneself is all important, because
without it, one cannot be friends with anyone else in
the world."*
-Eleanor Rooselvelt

Indulgence is not a bad word. Society has lead
us to believe that doing anything that just benefits us and no one else is bad. I beg to differ.
Personal time is a "must have," for a healthy
self image. Personal time is a safe self-indul-
gence as long as you don't put it before God
(like staying home on Sunday mornings to take
a leisure bubble bath during service). Scheduled personal time once a week or once a month
is reasonable and necessary.

Time alone allows you the opportunity to take
a step back from all the busyness of life, the
deadlines, projects and demands from your
family, career and friends. When you allot this
time to invest in yourself you are saying,

189

"Hey I'm important, I care about myself. I care about my body and my health."

I schedule into my planner little spurts of personal time each week. For example, every Thursday I get my hair done which takes approximately one hour. If you make regular beauty appointments, you'll experience a time of personal pampering that you deserve. Getting your hair and nails done weekly or bi-weekly will be relaxing and the image improvement will be rewarding.

One of my friends told me she uses grocery shopping as her get away time and she spends about thirty minutes reading magazines in the store.

Enjoy a massage from a professional masseuse. My husband and I along with some other friends spent a week once in Florida at the PGA Spa and Resort. We had full body massages and facials - the works. It was one of the most inspiring and relaxing vacations I ever took.

Your body will let you know when you need your private time. You'll be craving for a moment of solitude. Don't neglect the signals your body sends you. Instead, create a balance in your schedule. Don't wait for someone else to reduce your schedule for you, make time for yourself.

CHOOSE ONE ITEM FROM THIS LIST TO TAKE SOME PERSONAL TIME AND DO SOMETHING FOR YOURSELF EACH WEEK.

⌛ Enroll in a class to learn about a subject you've always been curious about.

⌛ Treat yourself to a make-over and buy some take home goodies.

⌛ Turn your bathroom into a spa. Escape for a few hours by bringing a few of your favorite magazines or books with you. Burn a scented candle and take a hot bubble bath. Dry off with a big fluffy towel and wrap yourself in a fluffy robe, then give yourself a facial.

⌛ Hire someone to clean your house for a month while you use that time to do something of your choice. (note: You may want to keep the housekeeper permanently.)

⌛ Meet a friend for lunch in an establishment that is relaxing and has ambiance.

⌛ Spend a few hours browsing in a book store. The best bookstores are those where you can sit down and read. Many bookstores now have cafes, to make your time there even more pleasurable.

POINTS OF MOTIVATION

☞Avoid burnout, schedule regular times to play.

☞Visit a nearby park, take a good book, sit in the sunlight and read.

☞Take a walk alone and enjoy the serenity. Think about exciting plans for your future.

☞Give yourself the freedom to do something you've always wanted to do...just for fun.

☞Check yourself into a luxury hotel, take a stack of magazines and indulge in reading and quiet time. I did this once with my decorating and travel magazines. What a great escape!

☞Sneak away to your bedroom, and relax in bed while catching up on some enjoyable reading.

My Motivational Journal

Imagine a full week with absolutely no obligations! A week devoted just to you. Explain in detail what you would do.

Take some of those ideas and schedule them in over the next few months.

#22
Think About
Positive Things

"Every thought is a seed sown, if allowed to fall into the mind, and to take root there, produces it's own. Good thoughts bear good fruit, bad thoughts bear bad fruit"
-James Allen

Three weeks had passed since I'd given birth to my son and second child, Ryan. I sat on the couch and sobbed uncontrollably thinking, "This should be the happiest time of my life. We've just moved into our new home, and I have a beautiful, perfectly healthy baby."

Instead of feeling the joys of parenthood, my mind was racing with negative thoughts. Wrapped in distraught and anger, I picked up the phone beside me and called my husband James at the office. I managed to contain myself while being cordial with his secretary, but once I heard his voice, I was flooded with emotion and burst into tears. Ever so calmly, he asked, "Honey what's going on? Is the baby all right?" "It's not the baby it's me!" I responded. "I feel so unhappy right now." Hearing my frustration, James said "take a deep breath, calm down and I will be home in twenty minutes." I sat there, hung up the phone, calmed down, and waited.

As James walked in, he embraced me. He spoke softly and sweetly; "Honey you are not thinking about positive things." "What positive things?" I questioned. "Your health, the baby's health, your progress and all the things God has promised you that has already come to pass," James replied with strength and motivation in every syllable. He looked into my eyes and asked, "Is this what they call postpartum blues?" "I guess so" I said, and we both laughed.

My husband came to my rescue by telling me that it was an attack from the devil and the result of long periods of sleep deprivation. He lovingly volunteered to take the night shift with our son so I could sleep.

In a matter of weeks I applied the word of God to my life, and began to think positively. I thought about things that were lovely like, decorating my new home; and things that are pure, like the word of God (it's the pure truth). As I did this, I was encouraged and motivated once again.

I criticized myself by thinking, I'm not supposed to get sad or disappointed, I'm a motivational speaker. Yet, the reality of the matter is, regardless of your position or calling in life, everyone has the opportunity to be sad or disappointed. How you choose to respond to the circumstances shows your attitude in life, and will determine the quality of your life-style.

The devil will try to attack you especially when you're weak in your flesh. Immediately after having a baby most women are weak in the flesh because their bodies have been through so much. However, if you stay focused on the word of God, you can maintain your motivation. After this incident I realized Satan's attacks and determined I would not be stopped. I pulled out every Christian video I had, and stacked all my Bible teaching tapes next to the couch with my tape recorder.

Over the course of the following weeks while I was recovering, I feasted on the word of God. The word of God is so full of life and victory, it will change your attitude. Turn to the Bible the next time you feel like saying something negative about yourself. Blast the thoughts of the enemy out of your mind. The most important opinion you will ever have of yourself doesn't come from others, it comes from you. Stay in the word of God so that your opinion of yourself lines up with what God says.

Many Christians have turned from positive thinking because they have allowed the New Age philosophy to steal the concept of positive thinking which originally came from God. Positive thinking begins with word of God. That's what Phillipians 4:8 is referring to; keep your thoughts positive. From now on, look at the bright side. Motivated people view setbacks as temporary events or opportunities to invent a new approach. If this isn't your natural way of thinking, then correct it by daily meditating on positive points from the word of God.

We spend one fifth of our lives talking, and speak enough words in one year to fill sixty-six books each eight hundred pages long. The average woman speaks thirty-thousand words a day. The more you talk, the greater the chance your words will get you into trouble. Ask the Holy Spirit to help you speak words to build up yourself and others, as well as control the thoughts behind your words. For out of the abundance of the heart, the mouth speaks.[1]

Points of Motivation

☞Be thankful for all the good in your life. As you go through your day, practice expressing your gratitude for all the acts of kindness you receive.

☞At bedtime each night, write in your journal one nice thing that happened to you during the day.

☞Say no to the news for one whole month and see how positive your thinking will be.

☞Eliminate negative converations with yourself and others. As soon as you hear negative words stop yourself and say, "No these words are destructive, I can't discuss this."

☞Be careful of sarcasm, cynicism and crticism. All are destructive. Don't target yourself or others with negative confessions.

☞Hold your tongue. When your emotions are fostering negative thoughts, learn to practice silence or you'll receive what you allowed to come out of your mouth.

☞ Quote positive scripture references when your mind is being bombarded with negative thoughts.

MY MOTIVATIONAL JOURNAL

What situation in your life can you use today to practice changing your negative thoughts to positive thoughts.

Write down ten positive thoughts about this situation.

#23
Listen to
Inspiring Music

"Take a music bath once or twice a week for a few seasons and you will find that it is to the soul what the water bath is to the body"
-Oliver Wendell Holmes

Music is a powerful vehicle. It can have a positive or negative effect on your emotional behavior. We've witnessed it's negative effect from all the news reports we have heard over the last decade about youth who have killed people, committed suicide and joined satanic cults because they claimed certain music lyrics drove them to do the things they really didn't want to do.

It's important that you monitor what you and your family listen to. Pay attention to the words and, be sure you are not playing music in your house that is blasting negative confessions.

203

If you can't understand the lyrics then read them. I've gotten wise over the years, before I purchase a new artist's cassette or compact disk, I look at the display copy and check out the words. You want to find out what the artist is trying to get across to his/her listeners.

When used properly, music can be very motivating. From the scripture reference I Sam. 16:23, we know that music has the ability to run off evil spirits or a bad mood.

In church the music should be positive and full of faith filled words. When the music is positive it alters the people's mood. It causes them to rejoice about the goodness of God. Pastor Rod Parsley sings a song at his church with the lyrics, " I got a promise, everything's going to be all right!" Now that's an encouraging song, because it's true, and it lines up with the word of God. You should consider investing in a collection of motivational music for your home and car.

To start your day off right, put in a good worship tape. Worship creates an atmosphere for focusing on God, it's one of the best ways to begin prayer or Bible study.

I'm writing at this point during the holiday season and good music just seems to go along with the holidays. As we were decorating our Christmas tree I said, "We need to keep Christmas music playing to set the mood."

To set the mood for cleaning the house, my housekeeper plays up tempo music. She says it motivates her to keep going. While you are studying or relaxing, play good classical music, it can stimulate your thinking.

One of the worst things you can do when you are feeling blue, is to listen to music that agrees with your situation. Sort through your music collection and check your inventory. Get rid of any music you isn't ministering positive words and encouragement into your life.

Points of Motivation

☞Visit a Christian bookstore and listen to a few artists before building your collection. Be sure to read the words so that you have a clear understanding of the artist's message.

☞Play a good worship tape first thing in the morning and see how it makes you feel.

☞Invest in a variety of good music: up tempo, mellow, classical, jazz, worship, and rap for the kids. Variety adds interest to your life. Don't get stuck with one type of music.

☞Try playing soothing music when it's time for the children to come home from school. It will change their attitude as they enter the house. You'll notice your children calming down and changing their tone and volume of voice.

☞Use music during your fellowship time with friends to set a comfortable atmosphere.

☞ Play good classical music while working on a project at home and watch how stimulated your thinking will be.

☞ Pick out music to fit the focus and theme of a special holiday or birthday and play the music for the whole family.

☞ Go to a symphony to observe the performance of classical music.

☞ Learn to play a musical instrument you've always wanted to play.

☞ Go see a musical artist perform live as often as possible for your enjoyment and entertainment.

MY MOTIVATIONAL JOURNAL

What made you choose the music you currently listen to?

What was the last song you heard that really moved you in a positive way?
What did it say?

#24
Take a
Tea Break

"There are a few hours in my life more agreeable
than the hour dedicated to the ceremony
known as afternoon tea."
-Henry James

For my daughter's eighth birthday she had a "star-studded" Tea Party sleep-over. She invited six of her dearest friends to a formal celebration. The young ladies came dressed in their Sunday clothes and fancy hairdos. It was a very beautiful party, one that every girl dreams of.

The lights were dimmed and the candles were lit. Next, the two servers poured each girl her tea and recited the evening's menu. While the young ladies were being served, the "tea chat" began. One girl said, "I'm so happy we're all together." "Well I'm just excited about the games

209

that are planned," said another. Their anticipation for the night's events was bubbling on the inside of them. I watched this friendly gathering as they began to calm down and simply enjoy their tea. I thought to myself how calming, yet stimulating the atmosphere was as they sipped their tea.

You don't need a lot of people to enjoy a lovely tea party. Whether you host a Victorian high tea or take a "just for me" solitary tea break, the luxury of sipping tea in a dainty, beautifully crafted tea cup is satisfying.

When you take time out to prepare a cup of tea just for you, it creates an enjoyable pampered feeling. You can make a motivating ritual out of tea, enjoying a quiet cup alone or hosting a tea party.

The purpose of a tea break is for reflection and intimacy. Alone, a tea break offers you a gracious time of meditation on your future. Sharing your tea time with someone else brings you together for meaningful conversation among friends. Tea is one of those subtle pleasures which enhances the quality of life with very little effort. A tea break doesn't have to be long, it can last anywhere from twenty minutes to one hour. No matter how much time you take, slow down and simply enjoy it to catch the calming effect a cup of tea can have.

Today, I was in a restaurant that sold little girls traveling tea party picnic baskets. It came complete with a tea set for two and a dainty pink picnic spread. Tea can also be a portable feast and wonderful for a romantic picnic with your husband or a simple time of sharing with a friend. What a way to add motivation to your day!

Take your tea party to the park or to the beach. You will have to brew the tea ahead of time or you could use a 100% juice drink as a substitute for tea. Don't forget to pack your tea sandwiches in a small cooler. Put all yourother items in a picnic basket and enjoy.

Recently, I purchased an authentic art deco styled Bistro set for my four seasons room. I placed it right in front of my windows overlooking the beautifully landscaped yard. This serves as a reminder to me to take time out from all the busyness of work to enjoy a restorative cup of tea. I have named this my think spot. Sitting at the little table with tea and a good book has become a rewarding ritual.

Mary Englebright says, "Tea is one of those simple luxuries like a good bar of chocolate or a good book, that truly enhances life with a minimum of fuss." To enjoy the simple pleasure in life is rewarding.

That's why I want to leave a legacy of tea time for my daughter Ariana. When she sighs, "I'm bored, let's go somewhere Mom." Often I'll say "Let's have a tea party!" Together we decorate our table, I brew the tea and sit down to chat. We share about her school events, future dreams or the latest book she's read. I believe a moment spent with a cup of tea gives us time to plan future dreams. I want to teach Ariana that quiet time can be motivating time.

Tea cups are also great collectibles. Ariana has a collection and so do I. To have your tea cups openly displayed serves as an inspiration and irresistible reminder to break for tea with the fond memories that accompany tea.

While writing this motivating point I'm sipping on a cup of peppermint tea, sorting through all of my books, articles, notes and quotes that I have collected about enjoying tea. By taking this short tea break, it's causes my creativity to surge.

Catch a few moments for yourself at least once a month to enjoy tea. Maybe when you come home from work, to help unclutter your mind. Another option is to take a cup of tea to bed with you, for a relaxing bedtime tradition. Pamper yourself for one weekend morning and put together a lovely tray of breakfast tea with a selection of fresh fruit and scones.

Having tea is so much fun. Make the time to enjoy it, alone or with family and friends.

POINTS OF MOTIVATION

☞Invite a friend to come over for tea and to bring along her photos and scrapbook. After enjoying your tea, play some relaxing music, work on your scrapbooks and talk.

☞Surprise your mate with a tea tray and goodies in bed.

☞Buy yourself a special "pick-me-up" tea cup and saucer. Display it openly and use it any time you need a pick up.

☞Host a formal tea party. Create a theme and invite some special friends over to enjoy.

☞Music provides a beautiful accompaniment to your tea, play classical music while having your tea break.

☞Serve your tea in the part of your house that stimulates you the most.

☞ Buy some books about tea. Read Emily

Barnes: *If Tea Cups Could Talk.*

☞Write an entry in your journal over a cup of tea.

☞Write a brief inspiring note to a friend over a cup of tea.

☞Read your Bible or a book of daily meditations. As you read and ponder, sip your tea.

☞Tea Party Idea: Have a tea party where each guest brings their favorite cup and shares why it is so special.

MY MOTIVATIONAL JOURNAL

Who would you like to have a tea party with? Write out your guest list.

What would you like to discuss with your friends? Be open and frank. This is a journal entry just for you.

#25
Practice
Journalizing

*"Keep a journal by your bedside. Million dollar
ideas often come at odd hours."*
-Stacia Pierce

A journal is a daily record of occurrences and observations. It's writing out the events in your life as you see them. A diary is geared more towards how you feel, though I do write how I feel in my journal along with that day's events. Personal reflection and self-initiated feedback can boost your motivation. Record in your journal what you want to be, do and have. You should make it a practice to write a journal entry every night as often as possible. Don't confine yourself to feeling like you're failing at journalizing if you miss a night's entry. When you take time to record what you want in your future, or what you want to change, then you are

217

in the process of developing the life you want. Note the activities of your day, what you've learned, ideas that come to you and the outcome received each day.

If you are feeling down when you are about to make an entry, begin your entry with; "Lord I thank you for..." When you change your thoughts to being grateful, your mood will improve. Write in your journal with an attitude of gratitude. Periodically you need to say and write, "I'm grateful for...my family, my spouse, my life, my church," etc., and then expand your thoughts.

A journal is a very private book and should be kept in a private place. You won't be open and honest in your writing, if you think someone might read your journal. Don't be afriad to write what you really feel. Don't censor your feelings. Put heart felt thoughts into your journal. The benefit of this honesty in your writing is that you can really identify yourself, and make positive changes where necessary. There is no formal way to journalize. Just write whatever comes to your mind. Sometimes my journal entry reads like a book and other times my thoughts are scattered. Many of my entries are creative ideas, so it reads more like an inventor's journal.

You can fill your journal with an assortment of lists. Lists help to keep us organized and focused. **An idea list** is where you record ideas that come to you for future projects and work related ideas. **A word list** is used whenever you find a new word to add to your vocabulary. List the word with a definition next to it and practice using it until it becomes a part of you.

Your journal is also an excellent place to record quotes that are relevant to you.

I keep my journal in a drawer at the head of my bed. Great ideas come at the strangest times. The same idea may never come again, so it is important to make a record of each idea right away. There have been many nights I've awaken from a dream on the way to the restroom and a God idea was impressed upon me.

Right away, I get out my journal and record it. Later, I may go back and elaborate on my thoughts concerning that idea.

Many days my entries read like a success journal. I record a goal that I've finally achieved or a quotation I read that applies to my life. Below are two entries from women who were compelled to keep journals after hearing me speak on the subject. I included one of my journal entries from my vacation while between New York and Philadelphia.

&Journal Entry Stacia Pierce   *8-27-97*

I'm visiting my cousins Sabrina and Wesley McGavock in Philadelphia. We have been vacationing for a few days now, shopping eating and sightseeing. We took the train over to Philadelphia. My feet were aching from walking so much, all I could think of was a good foot massage.

Since there was no possible way I would be getting one anytime soon, I grabbed my lotions and proceeded to massage my own feet. In doing so, I realized how neglected my feet had been. I was in desperate need of a pedi-cure. I began to mumble, "My feet look so bad, they didn't use to look like this"...then on the inside I heard the Spirit of the Lord say, whatever you neglect will deteriorate."

I began to think about children who get ne-glected. Then we wonder why they end up in gangs, on drugs, and dressing in 'grunge' clothes. Their self-esteem has deteriorated be-cause they've been neglected. When we ne-glect our purpose, the thing that God has cre-ated us for, then our lives begin to deterio-rate. Life then becomes useless. I think this entry is worth discussing in my book about pur-pose.
-Stacia Pierce

The names of the authors of the following journal entries have been deleted for reasons of privacy.

🖎 Journal Entry author #1   *1-7-98*
Sitting quietly and listening to other Chris-tian engage in conversation and not being able to participate had gotten tiring. The only way I felt I could fit in was to lie, making it seem as

though I knew what they were talking about or knew or experienced more than they did, when I had not. Not only did I feel embarassed because I felt they knew that I had lied, I knew that at that moment God was not pleased with me.

I found a scripture in Psalms that says; "Deliever my soul oh Lord from lying lips and from a deceitful tongue. I began to add this scripture into my prayer. My prayer had been answered by being a part of the Women's Wisdom Book Club. The more I read, the more knowledge I gained. The more knowledge I gained, the more interesting my conversation became, which ended my reason for lying.

Hosea 4:6 "My people are destroyed for a lack of knowledge."

✒️ Journal Entry author #2   *11-12-97*
Dear Heavenly Father;
Thank you so much for seeing to it that my family and I are here at LCCC. Here it has been one blessing after another. To some of my family and friends, my marriage and my

222

finances seem hopeless. But I can see how you are reconstructing, teaching, eliminating and adding things just as you please so that your will can take place in our lives. I am confident that because I serve you I won't be mocked by those skeptics. Since being here my marriage has experienced a major overhall. We've committed to better communication and are still growing closer via mutal goal setting, prayer and the ministry we receive.

Because of the constant improvements I see in my family circumstances I know you're answering my prayers. The faith message is so strong here and the leadership so sound. You are imparting into my family the rudiments for a successful Christian lifestyle. My husband is learning what true leadership is and it's making a difference in our relationship. I believe Lord that as he grasps the knowledge and understanding of it you'll honor his prayers and cause him to minister to the whole body of Christ.

Your journal lives and breathes the essence of who you are. Everyone should journalize.

POINTS OF MOTIVATION

☞Draw illustrations in your journal. You can include special mementos like a photo, a ticket or a pressed flower. You can tape them or leave them loose.

☞If you think what happens to you during a normal day is boring and not worth writing down, think again! In a few years you'll be glad you recorded these events. You never know, your daily stories may become a book one day.

☞Revert back to your childhood. Try adding stickers and magazine cutouts to your journal to give visual aids to your writing.

☞Use your journal to work through your thoughts. Write down your problems and feelings about the situation. Then write out your options.

☞Shop around for the best journal style that fits your personality. Find one that's nice enough for you to enjoy writing in it.

☞Determine your writing style. How will you approach your writing? You may want to divide your entries into sections with headings like: "News", "Today I learned..." and "Prayers." Or you could make entries of whatever comes to you. That's just the format I use.

☞Put a date and day with each entry. You'll want to be able to refer back to a specific event.

☞Don't try to write like an author or worry about incorrect spelling. You don't have to follow any rules.

☞Remember, journalizing is to free you, not to bind you. So your entries don't have to be made everyday.

☞Record your true feelings. This is your personal book. Keep it in a private place so you don't have to hold back when you write.

My Motivational Journal

What do you want to accomplish from keeping your journal?

What method of journalizing will you use? Explain.

My Motivational Notes

You seldomly remember everything you read. Use the following pages to record what you've learned. Jot down ideas, new words, quotes, etc.

_____

_____

_____

_____

_____

_____

_____

_____

_____

_____

_____

_____

_____

_____

_____

_____

_____

_____

My Motivational Notes

_____

_____

_____

_____

_____

_____

_____

_____

_____

_____

_____

_____

_____

_____

_____

_____

_____

_____

_____

_____

_____

My Motivational Notes

My Motivational Notes

My Motivational Notes

My Motivational Notes

My Motivational Notes

My Motivational Notes

A Final Word

Your motivation is your decision. Make the choice today to live the life you want. Now that you've read the book and have the tools, get started and get motivated!

Notes

#2 Laugh
1. McCalls October 1997.

#13 Browse Through your Photo Album
1. "Ways to Take Better Pictures"
   Family Circle Magazine 2/1/97, page 97
   Article by Joanne Van Zuidan.

#16 Listen to Inspiring Audio Tapes
1. Bio from, *How to be Happy Though Rich*
   by Revell Publishing. 1984 by Peter Daniels).

#22 Think About Positive Things
1. The Mother's Book of Wit & Wisdom
   Cheri Fuller Rav Press. 1995.

Other materials by Stacia Pierce

The Christian Women's Guide to Health and Nutrition
book

Soon to be Released:
How to Discover the Joy of Reading
book

Audio Cassette Series:
* How to Journalize   *2 tape series*

* The Joy of Reading   *Single cassette*

* The Disciplines of a Happy Home   *5 tape series*

* Attitudes of Achievers   *2 tape series*

* The Working Woman   *2 tape series*

The Prayer & Purpose Planner

I'd love to hear from you. I invite you to share your thoughts and comments concerning this book. Fondly, Stacia

To receive more information about additional materials by Stacia Pierce, or engage her for your church or women's program, please call or write:

**Life Changers Christian Center
808 Lake Lansing Road Suite 200
East Lansing, MI 48823
517-333-9860**

About the Author

Stacia Pierce is on a mission to attack mediocrity. She has a message of optimism that tells women there is greatness in them. Stacia focuses on the possibilities for women instead of the limitations. She illuminates purpose and direction in others and gives them the motivation to live above average.

Stacia is Editor-in-Chief of *W.O.R.D.* Magazine, founder of *Women of Royal Destiny Ministries*, director of a women's leadership team and on the advisory council of *Aspire* Magazine.

She has a heart for women and anyone exposed to her ministry will have their lives changed forever.

Stacia, her husband James and their two children: Ryan and Ariana reside in Lansing, MI.

Dr. DONSBACH tells you what
you always wanted to know about.....

HIGH
BLOOD
PRESSURE
(HYPERTENSION)

© 1993

KURT W. DONSBACH, D.C., N.D., Ph.D.

Published by
THE ROCKLAND CORPORATION
©1993

Printed in U.S.A.
ISBN 0-86664-057-6

From the Publisher:
This book does not intend to diagnose disease nor to provide specific medical advise. Its intention is solely to inform and to educate. The author and publisher intend that readers will use the information presented in this book in cooperation with a health professional.

Index

INTRO

It is obvious that an in-depth study of the circulatory system is not possible in this small booklet. However, by the time you have completed the reading of this, you will have a basic understanding of your internal plumbing, why so many people have problems with it and, even more important, how you can reduce your chances of developing problems or overcoming the ones you have existing in your blood vessel system.

THE HEART

At the center of the entire cardio-vascular (heart-blood vessel) system is the heart. it is a muscular organ with four chambers sealed off from each other by valves which work to control the blood flow throughout the internal areas of the heart. The blood which comes back to the heart is loaded with carbon dioxide and is routed to the lungs for an exchange of the carbon dioxide for oxygen, which is so essential for life. The oxygen-rich blood then goes back to the heart and is pumped out into the general circulation. The diagram which follows represents the flow of blood which travels an incredible 60,000 miles through a variety of large and very small blood vessels. The heart pumps the equivalent of 4,300 gallons of fluid in any given day with over 100,000 contractions in a 24 hour period.

This unceasing activity is an important factor in any heart related disorder. The heart is an organ that is in constant motion, expanding and contracting to produce a pumping action. It never rests, except between beats for a fraction of a second, and it thrives on motion. It demands the stimulation of body movement for several reasons, one of which is to prevent the infiltration of fat into the heart muscle, thus hindering its efficient operation. One must keep in motion as much as possible, exercising, walking, going up and down stairs, swimming, dancing, etc. Playing golf on weekends is not sufficient. There must be enough physical activity every single day to increase the heart rate above its normal 68-75 beats per minute. Many cardiologists are the opinion that "adequate" exercise means raising the pulse rate to above 120 beats per minute.

THE CIRCULATION: TWO-WAY NETWORK

The network pictured on the following page comprises some 60,000 miles of tubing which carries blood to every part of the body. Its most impressive feature is the circular manner in which it keeps the blood moving, always away from the heart in the arteries, and toward the heart in the veins - in spite of gravity and in spite of millions of alternate routes. The pump of the heart gives the flow its force, sending freshly oxygenated blood surging out the aorta, the body's largest artery, and into subsidiary arteries, even to the top of the head. The arteries branch out into smaller arterioles, which in turn branch out into millions of microscopic capillaries.

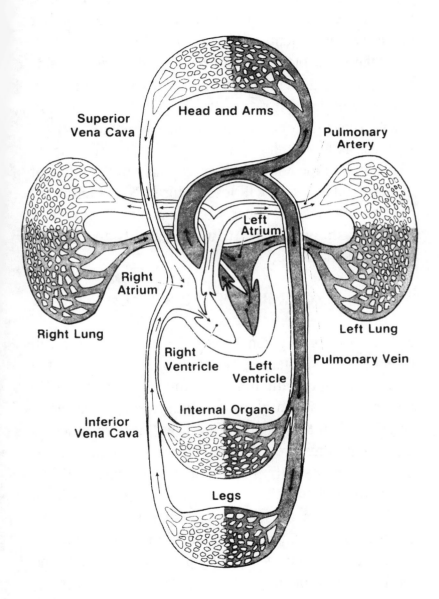

Superior Vena Cava

Head and Arms

Pulmonary Artery

Left Atrium

Right Atrium

Right Lung

Left Lung

Pulmonary Vein

Right Ventricle

Left Ventricle

Internal Organs

Inferior Vena Cava

Legs

Theses capillaries eventually unite to form venules, which unite into veins, thin-walled vessels with interior valves which prevent the blood from slipping backward. Thus the spent blood streams back to the heart. A side trip to the lungs, via a pulmonary network, refreshes it with oxygen, and it returns to the heart ready to start anew. The entire cycle takes less than a minute.

Exercise is an absolute must for the heart. The heart, like a limb of the body, must get its share of the effect of exercise, otherwise it will lose its tone. Non-exercise of the hand or foot will cause stagnation and atrophy. In a similar fashion, the heart lose its ability to respond unless it is in "shape."

YOUR BLOOD PRESSURE

Blood pressure is given by two figures (example: 120 over 80). It is obtained by inflating a cuff around the upper arm and reducing the compression until it is possible to hear the blood pumping through the blood vessel. When the sound is first heard, it is recorded as the systolic pressure. As the compression continues to decrease in the cuff, the sound fades away until no longer discernable. The reading at that point is known as the diastolic pressure. The systolic reflects the greatest amount of pressure in the blood vessel, literally during the ejection of pumping phase of the heart; and the diastolic represents the least amount of pressure, which occurs during the resting phase of the heart beat.

Although it is impossible to give a normal reading that applies to everyone, a good reading is about 120/80. This should not vary with age to any great degree - an upper normal limit would be 145/90, but I would only consider that normal if the individual were over 65 years of age. Here is a diagnostic tip I have learned over the years which is simple and will tell you a great deal about what is going on in your circulatory system.

Formula To Determine Work Load Of Heart
1. Record average pulse rate
2. Record average systolic blood pressure
3. Multiply pluse rate times systolic pressure
Normal: 8,000 to 9,500
Above 9,500: Suspect liver or kidney disease or atherosclerosis
Below 8,000: Suspect weak adrenals, weak musculature, nutrient deficiencies

NOTE: If diastolic pressure is above 90, suspect liver involvement, kidney problems or arteriosclerosis.

CONDITIONS WHICH AFFECT
BLOOD PRESSURE

There are many different conditions which may effect your blood pressure. It is my opinion that those which we will list as being nutritionally related may often be the ones which are the most important.

STRESS - A spat with your spouse, employer or children will temporarily raise your blood pressure. So will financial problems, fear and other emotional factors which bring the sympathetic nervous system into play. This sympathetic response will activate the adrenal glands to produce a hormone which tightens up or narrows the diameter of the blood vessels. Physiologically speaking, this is a defense mechanism to enable you to function more efficiently by increasing the amount of oxygen and nutrients available to all tissue cells. Such a temporary increase in blood pressure will not be harmful unless you already have high blood pressure, in which case it could bring about a stroke. This is why chronic hypertensive individuals are always told by their doctor to stay clam and not get too excited.

SMOKING - Within seconds after you light up, your blood pressure increases as much as 15-20 points. This action comes from the stimulant effect nicotine has on the adrenal glands which send out a hormone to help defend the body against this deadly toxin. The blood vessels constrict and the pressure goes up!

In the heavy smoker, this constant stimulation with resultant constriction of blood vessels eventually pro-

10.

duces a chronic or lasting constricting of the small blood vessels in the extremities. From this, we get decreased oxygen and nourishment supply to the areas normally supplied by these capillaries, and a slow degeneration sets in. Eventually, a serious complicated condition known as Buerger's Disease can come about. One of the treatments of Buerger's Disease is amputation of the limb involved. That should be reason enough to refrain from smoking.

SODIUM CHLORIDE - Common ordinary table salt can affect your blood pressure tremendously. We have many chemical balances which normally work in our body to maintain good health. One of these is the "sodium-potassium pump." Potassium is a mineral which normally is quite concentrated within the cell and sodium is concentrated in the extra-cellular fluids. These two minerals have a system of alternately bringing nutrients into the cell and discharging wastes from the cell. However, if sodium becomes excessive, wastes cannot be discharged from the cell properly and nutrients do not enter properly. Both the extra and intra-cellular fluids increase, and a condition known as dropsy or edema occurs. This creates extra pressure on the thousands of miles of blood vessels, which automatically increases the pressure inside the blood vessel and you have hypertension as a result.
The use of chemical diuretics can bring about this condition by lowering the potassium level. Please note

that I am well aware the common treatment of high blood pressure includes the use of chemical diuretics - in all such cases, a great deal of attention should be given to the supplementation of potassium to the diet. The use of diuretics treats on of the symptoms (edema) rather than the cause, which may be a sodium-potassium imbalance.

KIDNEY DISEASE - Kidney disease brings about hypertension in a similar fashion as a sodium-potassium imbalance would. The kidneys are unable to eliminate the liquid wastes from the body and they accumulate, producing edema and toxicity. Excessive smoking, a poor diet, excessive coffee and/or tea drinking are all contributing factors to kidney disease.

LIVER CONGESTION - All the blood in the body flows through the liver, both for detoxification and to pick up nutrients which the liver stores. If the liver is congested with toxins or chemicals, overridden with fatty degeneration, or has lost its ability to function properly because of continual abuse by alcohol and has become hardened, a back pressure builds up in the portal circulation which can be reflected in the whole body circulation as hypertension. It has been my experience that liver congestion may be a common cause of high blood pressure, and my contention is backed by hundreds of patients who no longer suffer from hypertension because of treatment directed toward restoring liver function. Always remember that the liver is the master chemist in the body.

ATHEROSCLEROSIS - ARTERIOSCLEROSIS

We must not overlook what many feel is the major cause of high blood pressure - the narrowing of the arterial system by deposits of calcium, cholesterol, fibrin, and other blood constituents in what is commonly referred to as atherosclerosis or arteriosclerosis. This condition, which is most likely caused by a disease of the wall of the blood vessel which causes a rupture of the inner lining (which the body immediately repairs to protect you from internal bleeding) and creates a perfect circumstance for the formation of plaque. Plaque is a combination of cholesterol, calcium, triglycerides, blood proteins, etc. which attach themselves to the fibrin which the body used to plug up the tear in the wall. (For further information, read my booklet on "Oral Chelation.") As this plaque formation increases, the internal diameter of the blood vessel is decreased considerably, which will result in increased pressure because we are forcing the same amount of fluid through a smaller pipe.

TUMORS - In a very small proportion of high blood pressure patients, other factors, such as tumors, are involved. Most of these are really surgical cases and do not properly come under this discussion.

NUTRIENT DEFICIENCIES - In the second half of this book, we will go into quite some detail on the effect that calcium, magnesium, potassium and other nutrient deficiencies have on creating the condition of hypertension.

NOW I KNOW WHY, BUT. . . .

Probably more readers are interested in knowing what to do about high blood pressure than in what causes it. I must begin by saying that it is important to understand the seriousness of the condition to be properly motivated to elimiate the cause. Study the following charts and recognize the impact that your blood pressure can have on your life.

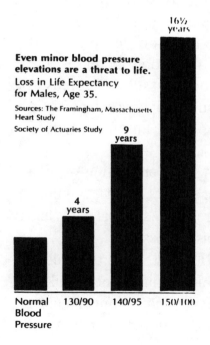

Even minor blood pressure elevations are a threat to life.
Loss in Life Expectancy for Males, Age 35.

Sources: The Framingham, Massachusetts Heart Study

Society of Actuaries Study

16½ years

9 years

4 years

Normal Blood Pressure   130/90   140/95   150/100

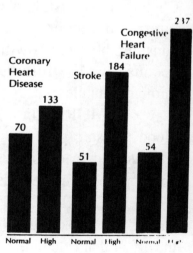

Coronary Heart Disease

Stroke

Congestive Heart Failure

70   133   51   184   54   2 37

Normal   High   Normal   High   Normal   High

Number of Patients With Normal and High Blood Pressure

14.

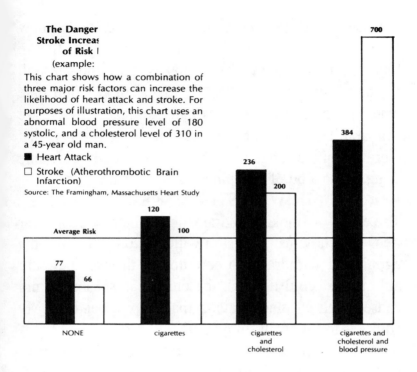

The Danger
Stroke Increas
of Risk !
(example:

This chart shows how a combination of three major risk factors can increase the likelihood of heart attack and stroke. For purposes of illustration, this chart uses an abnormal blood pressure level of 180 systolic, and a cholesterol level of 310 in a 45-year old man.

■ Heart Attack

□ Stroke (Atherothrombotic Brain Infarction)

Source: The Framingham, Massachusetts Heart Study

700

384

236

200

120

Average Risk   100

77

66

| NONE | cigarettes | cigarettes and cholesterol | cigarettes and cholesterol and blood pressure |

OVERCOMING STRESS

We discussed stress as being a factor in hypertension, although not a major one, in my opinion. Unless the stress is continuous, it will not create the sustained, dangerous high blood pressure which kills or cripples. Adequate rest often helps in relieving tension, and there is more than adequate evidence that well nourished individuals respond to stress with less physical strain. Meditation, properly carried out, can be one of the most positive answers to eliminating stress from ones life that exists. There are so many good audio and video tapes on this subject, that I can only encourage you to invest

15.

in some of them and enjoy their benefits. Another new answer is the use of a flashing light device that fits on like a pair of glasses. This relaxes the mind through rhythmic pulsations to enter the "alpha" or peaceful state where restoration and healing can take place. These are available from select companies, but I have found that there is quite a range of prices for essentially the same thing, so do a bit of shopping before investing.

HOW TO STOP SMOKING

The effect of smoking is dramatic on the blood vascular tree. But how can one stop without going through the agonies of withdrawl so common to drugs? Few are able to go "cold turkey", the change is so abrupt and causes such an inner craving that help is needed. My advise is to follow this program.

1. Procure a medication called diphenyl hydantoin sodium, more commonly sold as Dilantin® (USA), or Fenidantoin® (Mexico). Take 100 mg three times daily and within less than 10 days, you will usually have given up cigaretts painlessly. The drug is one of the more safe drugs in the pharmacopia and using it for one month, which is what I recommend, is not going to be harmful. It is a prescription drug in the United States, but it can be procured from Pharmaceuticals International, P.O. Box 638, Rosarito Beach, Baja, Mexico without a prescription. A one month supply is approximately $12 (90 tablets) and that is usually all it takes.

2. Since smoking is a habit deeply associated with stress, use destressing aids such as audio and video tapes which are readily available. The secret is to set aside at least 30 minutes or more each and every day to listen and watch these tapes.

3. Exercise daily for 30 minutes or more. Walking is just fine, but competitive sports such as tennis, which involve others, might be better in this case.

4. Use good foods in your diet, staying away from the coffee and alcohol which normally trigger the use of cigarettes. Get in the habit of using an excellent quality multi-vitamin-mineral combination as a supplement every meal.

Thirty days of this regime and the chances of your smoking ever again are close to nil.

SODIUM CHLORIDE SUBSTITUTE

Since the use of sodium chloride is a definite factor in high blood pressure, I highly suggest that you eliminate it completely from your kitchen cupboard. Many are able to enjoy the flavor of food without the use of this substance and have not difficulty in adapting. Some may feel they wish to use a flavoring or seasoning agent, and for them, I suggest the following:

A mixture of potassium chloride, sodium chloride, kelp, calcium carbonate, magnesium carbonate, lysine and silica. This product offers more than flavoring, it is literally a nutritional supplement!

17.

The flavor enhancement that it offers is very similar to that of regular "salt," but the sodium chloride content has been reduced by 65%.

NOTE: I do not recommend the products which are marketed as "sea salt" or "earth salt" since they are almost pure sodium chloride, which is what you want to reduce.

ASSISTING THE KIDNEYS

Although there are a variety of kidney diseases, all of them are benefited by an increased consumption of fluids, particularly water. It is suggested that *all* coffee, tea, alcohol and high sugar containing beverages be discontinued if you have kidney disease.

You may have to force yourself to drink water for a short period, but soon you will find that you prefer this "universal solvent." Some may wish to drink distilled water; if you do so, be sure to supplement with a broad spectrum mineral formula, as distilled water is an unsaturated solution and will tend to take minerals out of your body.

Never use tap water. The contaminants in tap water today are so numerous that you should really read my booklet entitled "Water" for more information. Most people forget that avoiding drinking tap water is just part of the solution. Bathing in tap water for a period of 20 minutes will allow your body to absorb the equivalent of drinking two quarts of that same water! So in order to be really safe, and particularly if you have

18.

kidney disease, do not drink or bathe in tap water. Many have found that the use of a whole house bone charcoal filtration system is the answer, or if you live in an apartment, you can get a separate sink and bath units that attach to the spigot and effectively filter the water. Bone charcoal has emerged as the filtration media of choice, since it is the only media that removes the heavy metals associated with causing hypertension. The investment for these units, ranging from $400 for an apartment to $700 for a whole house system, are inconsequential when measured against good health.

Another suggestion for those with kidney disease is the use of the Liver-Kidney-Bowel Cleansing Fast, outlined later. It is an excellent means of restoring kidney function. Try it!

OVERCOMING LIVER CONGESTION

Liver involvement in hypertension is often overlooked, in my opinion. In order to decongest the liver, it is necessary to abstain from solid foods for a few days. The Liver-Kidney-Bowel Cleansing Fast outlined later is an absolute must for any patient who wishes to see results quickly in hypertension. Since the program is detailed later, I will not enlarge here, but after you are off the fast, I suggest you use some herbs to create a continuation of the cleansing process. Herbs are natures medicines and are very effective in accomplishing cleansing throughout the entire body. I use a combination of several herbs, all of which have complimentary cleansing properties. They include garlic, quassia, black cohosh, chaparral, fenugreek, red sage and golden seal. This combination is available as a single formula from your health food store.

The use of some of these, such as garlic, have a long term history in folk medicine for the treatment of high blood pressure, have withstood the test of time and are quite inexpensive and safe. The importance of this continued cleansing cannot be emphasized too much, in hypertension there are degenerative changes which have taken place and the liver is the single most important organ in re-establishing normal body chemistry.

After completeing the cleansing fast, your next step is to use the Creative Restoration Diet as your guideline in eating habits for the rest of your life. It is an enjoyable, healthy way to choose and combine foods. Regarding supplements, the B-complex vitamins will help to hasten the recovery of your liver, as well as provide insurance against future occurrences. It is my opinion that the B-complex factors should be taken in combination with a total vitamin-mineral supplement for best results.

ATHEROSCLEROSIS - ARTERIOSCLEROSIS

Since a decrease in the diameter of a blood vessel will produce high blood pressure, we should explore means of reducing such accumulations inside the walls of the arteries. There are, interestingly enough, several effective methods of cleansing the arteries.

INTRAVENOUS CHELATION

This is a method of introducing into the blood stream a synthetic amino acid which has the chemical property of binding deposited calcium and other minerals and carrying it out of the body via the urine. When the calcium is picked up from the blood vessel wall, it disrupts the other accumulated materials (cholesterol, triglycerides, etc.) and thus clears the channel and automatically lowers the blood pressure because of a larger diameter in the artery. Check with your local health food store for the name of a doctor who uses this procedure. Chelation offers a new direction for advanced clogging of the arteries, since it influences the basic pathology taking place. The surgical procedure to replace arteries does not in any way stop the disease process progression in other areas of the body.

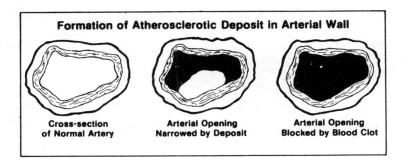

Formation of Atherosclerotic Deposit in Arterial Wall

| Cross-section of Normal Artery | Arterial Opening Narrowed by Deposit | Arterial Opening Blocked by Blood Clot |

CHELATION

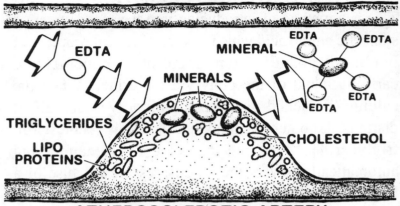

ATHEROSCLEROTIC ARTERY

ORAL CHELATION

The use of a special oral formula can accomplish benefits similar to intravenous chelation in less serious cases of hypertension, but it may take a little longer. This fomula was so successful in lowering blood pressure and restoring circulation, that it has become the most copied nutritional formula of all times. I cannot say enough good things about this formula, which has been reprinted for your convenience in the latter part of this book.

REMOVING TUMORS

A tumor of the kidneys or adrenals can cause hypertension. These are ususally non-malignant and are the cause of only a very few cases of high blood pressure. The surgical removal of such a tumor will relieve the blood pressure and a proper diet and supplement program can help prevent such a recurrence.

22.

ANOTHER LOOK AT SALT

Oregon researcher David McCarron and co-workers, have told America what it wants to hear: "People who eat salt and dairy products have lower blood pressure than those who don't." Immediately after the announcement, the guardians of American health moved to plug the public's ears; the American Heart Association, among others, warned hypertensives not to relax their vigil against salt. But the report is most interesting. The group's methods and some of their results leave something to be desired, say many scientists, but the concept - that our single minded paranoia about salt is wrong - could be right.

The prevailing anti-salt obsession is based mostly on studies showing that populations, such as the Yanamamo Indians of Brazil, who eat virtually no salt, have almost no cases of high blood pressure. But scientists haven't been able to prove that people with hypertension consume excessive salt, and low-salt diets don't always reduce blood pressure. Still, health policy makers have urged American to shun their shakers in the hopes of preventing hypertension in the estimated, an unidentified, 15 percent whose blood pressures may be salt sensitive. Even so, plenty of researchers still doubt the value of salt starvation.

McCarron, director of the hypertension program at Oregon Health Sciences University, is among those who believe most people shouldn't deprive their taste buds. His previous views that calcium may be more important than sodium in regulating blood pressure have brought accusations of influence by the dairy industry, which provides about six percent of his budget. The current study was not funded by dairy interests.

In their recent report, McCarron, Cynthia Morris, Holly Henry, and John Stanton used data from a 1974 federal survey of 20,749 Americans. Volunteers were given a medical examination and asked about their diets. Each reported what he or she had eaten in the past 24 hours, and this information was broken down into 17 nutrients.

Excluding those under 18, pregnant women, known hypertensives, and those on a low-salt diet, the scientists were left with data for 10,372 people. Of these, 9.2 percent unknowingly had hypertension. These people consumed about 20 percent less calcium, 14 percent less potassium, and 12 percent less sodium than those with normal blood pressure. The researchers conclude that a person who eats few dairy products, which contain all three nutrients, is more likely to have high blood pressure.

"My concern is that we shouldn't just tell everyone to cut out salt." says McCarron. "This data says it's not that simple. Calcium appears to be the driving force, but it won't work unless there's adequate potassium and sodium in the diet. People who cut out salt may inadvertently cut out calcium."

But McCarron's sodium findings are muddied, claim other researchers, because the "24-hour recall" method of determining diet may be unreliable. Calcium and

24.

potassium can be estimated from such reports, says hypertension specialist Harriet Dustan of the University of Alabama, but not sodium. There is no way to account for the salt used in food preparation or at the table. And the scientists say people tend not to remember all they eat, especially items such as salty snacks. Previous research has found that at least a week of reports are necessary to establish what a person really eats.

"The method definitely underestimates, but not in a consistent way," says Gerald Payne of the National Heart, Lung and Blood Institute. "So McCarron's conclusions about sodium and blood pressure are inappropriate."

McCarron maintains that the underestimation is consistent. He cites studies showing that people who tend to salt their food also choose salty food. The numbers may be wrong, he says, but the trend is right. Moreover, his group has preliminary results showing that rats fed low-salt, low-calcium diets have higher blood pressure than those on high-salt, high-calcium diets.

What's good about McCarron's study, say its critics, is that it indicates a relationship between calcium, potassium, and sodium in regulating hypertension. It supports studies in which calcium and potassium appear to lower blood pressure. There is also evidence that calcium and sodium may interact in constricting and relaxing blood vessels and, other research indicates that as the ratio of sodium to potassium rises, so does blood pressure. The publicity the study has received, suggests some, may help defuse the mythology surrounding sodium as the sole actor in blood pressure.

"He's done a terrific thing," says Cornell University's Michael Alderman, who nevertheless disagrees with the sodium results. "He shows that when you alter the diet for one nutrient, you change others, which may have a negative effect. He makes the point that focusing on sodium alone makes it appear to be the sole issue in blood pressure. And that's too simplistic."

POTASSIUM FOR HYPERTENSION?

A banana a day - or better yet, two or three bananas, a large potato, some orange juice, and a bite or two of melon - could keep the doctor away when hypertension is the problem, a University of Minnesota researcher contends.

Such high potassium diets were standard fare for prehistoric hunter-gatherers and probably account for their virtual absence of hypertensive disease among their counterparts in remote areas of the world today, notes Dr. Louis J. Tobian Jr., a professor of medicine and chief of the university's hypertension section.

"Among hypertensive rats fed potassium supplements, deaths from stroke and kidney failure declined dramatically, even when blood pressures remained high," Dr. Tobian told science writers at an American Heart Association forum.

The Minnesota group first looked at the effects of high

potassium intake on renal lesions of Dahl S rats, a strain genetically programmed to develop salt-induced hypertension. After 24 weeks, rats given a moderately high sodium (4%) diet without potassium supplements developed significanly more focal tubular dilation and greater reduction in renal capillary plasma flow than did rats given the same amount of salt with either 3.8% potassium citrate or 2.6% potassium chloride.

On the basis of those results, the researchers turned to a breed of stroke-prone, spontaneously hypertensive rats to see if potassium supplementation might similarly protect cerebral arteries from hypertensive damage. After four months on a 0.75% potassium, 4% sodium diet, 20 of 24 rats had died. In contrast, only one of 50 rats given 2.11% potassium and the same amount of salt had died during that time.

When the studies were repeated with Dahl S rats, mortality was 4% for the potassium group was 55% for the unsupplemented group.

"What's more," notes Dr. Tobian, "four surviving stroke-prone rats on the "normal potassium" diet had evidence of brain hemorrhage, whereas none of the 34 rats on high potassium did. It thus appears that a high potassium diet allows brain arteries to carry a usually damaging level of intra-arterial pressure without damaging the arterial wall," he says.

"Because blacks in the southeastern U.S. are known to have high stroke and kidney failure rates, coupled with low potassium intake," says Dr. Tobian, "potassium supplements might be protective for them."

An epidemiologic survey of 2,500 blacks and whites in three U.S. cities adds weight to his premise. In 1978, Dr. George D. Miller, of the Johns Hopkins School of Hygiene and Public Health, found that blacks with higher potassium intake did, in fact, appear to be protected against the hypertensive effect of salt, making it almost a moot entity.

URINARY POTASSIUM INVERSELY PROPORTIONAL TO BLOOD PRESSURE

There appears to be a significant negative correlation between blood pressure levels and urinary potassium values, two physicians agreed at a symposium on potassium in cardiovascular and renal medicine presented by the Johns Hopkins University School of Medicine.

"The sodium/potassium ratio also determined blood pressure," said Dr. W. Gordon Walker, professor of medicine and director of the renal division at the University.

In Dr. Walker's study of 574 normotensive and hypertensive subjects, 21 to 58 years old, a significant inverse relationship was found between recumbent diastolic blood pressure and urinary potassium. Urinary potassium values differed significantly among the subjects, but their urinary sodium values were similar. Differences in the sodium/potassium ratios were due to the variations in potassium, Dr. Walker commented. In a study by other investigators of populations in six geographic areas of Japan, an inverse relationship was found between hypertension prevalence and serum potassium levels, indicating that the higher the level of potassium, the lower the blood pressure.

In a separate presentation, Dr. Christopher J. Bulpitt, of the London School of Hygiene and Tropical Medicine, said that the results of population studies show a positive association between sodium intake and hypertension, but suggests a negative relationship between potassium intake and blood pressure.

The results of population studies within a country, which are less subject to the variables that affect several country studies, also show a negative correlation between blood pressure values and plasma potassium.

With all this evidence staring us in the face from multiple sources, why has the medical stand been adamant about the use of medication, rather than trying to balance the sodium/potassium levels?

DIURETIC USE MAY RESULT IN TOTAL BODY POTASSIUM DEPLETION

"The long-term use of kiuretics in high doses may result in total body potassium depletion," Dr. Trefor Morgan said at a symposium on potassium in cardiovascular and renal medicine presented by the Johns Hopkins University School of Medicine. He stated that contrary to popular opinion, potassium chloride supplementation in patients on diuretics does not correct the potassium deficiency because there is often an associated magnesium deficiency which will halt the proper absorption of potassium.

He stated that the first step in the treatment of hypertension should be to reduce the patient's sodium intake and to increase the potassium intake. All of this falls into the same sort of advise that one would conclude from all the other studies and offers a reasonable alternative to the diuretic drug therapy so popular in the medical field.

CALCIUM SUPPLEMENTATION EFFECTIVE IN HYPERTENSION

"Oral calcium supplementation is an effective and well tolerated treatment for mild to moderate hypertension," says Dr. Cynthia D. Morris of Oregon Health Sciences University in Poland.

Thirteen of twenty-eight hypertensive patients responded to 8 weeks of calcium carbonate therapy with a 13% decline in standing systolic and a 9% drop in diastolic blood pressure. Calcium was more effective in hypertensives than in normotensive control subjects. Only 5 of 30 control subjects had significantly lower blood pressure during the active treatment phase of the double-blind, placebo-controlled, cross-over study.

The side effects of one gram of calcium from calcium carbonate per day for 8 weeks were non-existent, and obviously far less than what would have been experienced if diuretics had been used.

In the 13 hypertensive responders, calcium was associated with a reduction in mean standing blood pressure from 152/95 to 132/88. The mechanism responsible for the reduction was not determined, nor was there any way to tell which individual would respond. The most likely answer lies in calcium's ability to decrease vascular smooth muscle tone, which might be abnormally increased due to hormonal influences of stress, etc. Epidemiologists have noted a lower prevalence of hypertension in persons with a higher calcium intake over the years.

In another study in New York, calcium was also able to significantly lower blood pressure. Diastolic blood pressure dropped in 16 of 26 patients with mild essential hypertension treated only with calcium supplements for six months, according to investigators at Cornell University Medical College.

Reporting the results of the uncontrolled trial to the American College of Cardiology, Dr. Lawrence M. Resnick said the mean blood pressure for the entire group dropped from 161/94 at the start of the trial to 154/89 after six months. But, among the 16 responders, diastolic pressure dropped 10 points or more, noted Dr. Resnick, an assistant professor of medicine. The decline was greatest in patients with low initial serum ionized calcium levels.

The Cornell team investigated calcium's potential anti-hypertensive effect among outpatients after an earlier five day inpatient study demonstrated that calcium loading under metabolic balance conditions lowered blood pressure in some patients.

In the outpatient study, patients were evaluated after a three week washout period of no anti-hypertensive medication. Baseline levels of serum ionized calcium and magnesium, plasma renin activity, and a 24 hour urinary excretion of sodium, potassium, calcium, magnesium, and aldosterone were measured. At the start of the trial and monthly during the study, diastolic and systolic blood pressures were measured with patients in the supine, seated and upright positions.

Patients with a history of kidney stones or basal hypercalciuria were excluded from the trial, leaving 26 who were treated with 2 grams of calcium carbonate in divided doses four times daily. They were instructed not to reduce salt intake or otherwise modify their diets for the six month period.

"In addition to serum ionized calcium level, sodium balance predicted whether a patient would respond to therapy," said Dr. Resnick. Patients with low starting levels of serum ionized calcium and higher average urinary sodium excretion rates - who presumably ate more salt - responded to oral calcium with lower diastolic pressures.

In contrast, non-responders tended to have higher starting levels or serum ionized calcium and lower urinary sodium excretion rates. Calcium therapy actually increased diastolic pressure 5% to 10% in some of these patients, Dr. Resnick said. This would act as a clear guideline to the health practitioner who could now make an intelligent decision as to whether the patient might respond or not by simply looking at the blood test results.

Most importantly, no patients experienced adverse effects that would have necessitated calcium withdrawl, and none complained of lethargy or sexual dysfunction, two well known side effects of the drugs commonly used in hypertension.

A speculation that comes from all this research is that black hypertensives might respond very well to calcium therapy because of their high incidence of lactose intolerance which would decrease their absorption of calcium from the richest source - dairy products.

Another benefit could be associated with calcium supplementation, in that the study demonstrated a gradual reduction of pressure which was still going on when the study was concluded at the end of six months. This could mean that extended supplementation would continue to lower the pressure to the normal range over a period of time.

As we have indicated, the precise mechanism by which calcium lowers blood pressure isn't clear, but we speculate that is relaxes the muscle layer in the artery. The Cornell team which conducted this research believes that calcium acts as a calcium blocker by competing with the hormone 1,25-dihydroxy vitamin D. "We've found that 1,25-dihydroxy vitamin D administration will undo calcium effects on blood pressure," Dr. Resnick said, "so we think calcium is suppressing the action of 1,25-dihydroxy vitamin D."

MAGNESIUM - AN OVERLOOKED FACTOR

Should magnesium supplementation be routine for the prevention of sudden death in patients with ischemic heart disease? Does diuretic induced hypomagnesia interfer with the effectiveness of anti-hypertensive drugs? Are some of the kidney and inner ear toxic effects of some medications due to an alteration in cell membrane permeability that results from magnesium deficiency?

All good questions, and all questions which are being researched and hopefully answered. The frequency of magnesium deficiency was not appreciated in medical circles until recent advances in atomic absorption spectrometry and its use in some clinical laboratories. What is even more significant is that major diseases, for which little answers were known, may in fact respond to increasing the amounts of this key intracellular mineral.

"Magnesium may play an important role in blood pressure control," says Dr. Robert Whang, Professor of Medicine at the University of Oklahoma Health Sciences Center, as a result of a study on the prevalence of magnesium and potassium deficiencies in 1,000 treated hypertensives at the VA Medical Center in Oklahoma City. He found that patients with magnesium deficiency, regardless of the level of potassium, required a greater number of drugs for the same degree of blood pressure control than did those with normal magnesium levels. "We're beginning to think of the possibility that whenever there's a potassium deficient patient, the clinician might be well advised to pay attention to the magnesium," said Dr. Whant. That leads us to recommending not only potassium and maybe calcium, but also magnesium. A deficiency of magnesium allows more calcium to bind to the surface of the cell, including nerve and smooth muscles, which produces more contraction of the arteries, including blood pressure.

A recent article in the *American Heart Journal* suggest that magnesium deficiency can precipitate ventricular fibrillation and result in sudden death in patients with acute ischemic heart disease.

One well recognized researcher in cardiovascular problems has stated that, without any question, magnesium supplementation reduces myocardial necrosis (heart muscle death) and other deadly changes that occur in a heart attack. The question that must be answered is: Why is there, as of yet, very little support for magnesium therapy in ischemic heart disease?

Serious arrhythmias (irregular beating of the heart) that are drug resistant often respond well to magnesium, as researched by Johns Hopkins University.

Other studies show that magnesium loss induced by certain drugs caused serious side effects such as kidney toxicity and hearing damage.

All of this would have one concerned that the medical profession has not yet "discovered" magnesium and claimed it as a wonder drug. The problem may lie in the fact that magnesium is not able to be patented and it is comparatively inexpensive, so there is very little big money to be made on it. This, of course, applies to all the nutrients we have been discussing here.

If one were to look in old pharmacopia volumes, you would find that since 1925, it has been known that pharmacologic doses of magnesium salts can produce hypotension in normotensives and lower high blood pressure in hypertensives.

Many patients need for anti-hypertensive drugs have been totally eliminated by the use of magnesium in supplemental form. Several recent studies point to a relationship between hypertension and decreased magnesium concentration in blood and tissues, and the fact that hypertension rates climb in areas with magnesium-poor soil or soft drinking water.

MAGNESIUM - MORE EVIDENCE

When the magnesium content of isolated coronary, cerebral, and peripheral blood vessels is lowered artificially, rapid contractile responses result in humans and animals. These lowered magnesium levels potentiate the action of a group of neurohumoral constrictors, including adrenergic amines and angiotensin (these substances tend to tighten the blood vessels). Further evidence of magnesium's role in regulating vasomotor tone is seen in animals when the spontaneous tone of arteries and veins is inhibited by an excess of magnesium in the blood stream. This results in a decreased arterial resistance to blood flow.

Some types of hypertension are due to direct effects of

hypomagnesium on arteriolar and venule tone. The low blood magnesium content produces progressive vasoconstriction of the arterioles, precapillary sphincters, and microcirculatory venules. Eventually, overall systemic resistance increases; capillary flow is curtailed and the end result is hypertension.

In studies done on rats, when the diet was deficient in magnesium, the blood pressure rose as much as 32 points over rats fed a diet adequate in magnesium. All of the magnesium deficient rats had constricted blood vessels and the more severe the deficiency of magnesium, the more restricted the blood vessels. On severely deficient diets, the constriction was as much as 33%, while moderately deficient diets produces a 13% reduction in lumen size.

All of this information leads us to confirm the fact that magnesium is important to keep calcium in control, since magnesium regulates the entry and exit of calcium into the cell. When magnesium is deficient, calcium influx is enhanced, causing contraction of the muscle cell particularly.

AUTHOR'S NOTE:

Every so often, a particularly good article comes along that is worthy of reprinting in its entirety. The following is such and I present it as another "proof" of the importance of nutrition in hypertension.

CLINICAL SIGNIFICANCE OF DIURETIC INDUCED MAGNESIUM LOSS

by Thomas Dyckner, M.D., Ph.D., and
Per Olov Wester, M.D.

Several factors influence the renal handling of magnesium, among which is medication with diuretic drugs. The loop-blocking diuretics exert their action in the ascending limb of Henle's loop of the kidney and, not surprisingly, cause massive losses of magnesium from the body. The exact mechanism by which these losses occur is unclear, but they seem to be related in some way to the simultaneous losses of sodium, chloride, and water.

The thiazide diuretics are active in a somewhat more distal site of the nephron, where only small amounts of magnesium are normally reabsorbed. The use of this type of drug leads to an initial increase in loss of renal magnesium, but later, the excretion often returns to values within the so-called normal range. In many patients on chronic thiazide therapy, however, elevated magnesium excretion persists. The explanation for this is not clear, but may be related to derangements of extracellular volume or aldosterone secretion or to changes in extracellular calcium levels and parathyroid-hormone secretion.

Several studies dealing with the urinary excretion of magnesium following diuretic therapy have demonstrated magnesium loss increases of 25 to 50 percent. In short-term experiments with high doses of loop-blocking diuretics, increases of close to 400 percent have been observed.

The impact of these continuing losses on tissue magnesium content is disputed. Studies of weeks or months usually show no change in tissue magnesium following diuretic therapy. Long-term investigations, however, demonstrate that there is a successive loss of magnesium from the body, which may attain significant levels.

Especially at risk for developing a magnesium deficiency are elderly patients, who often have an insufficient dietary intake of magnesium and may have compromised absorption from the gastrointestinal tract. These patients are often treated with higher doses of diuretics; the more potent loop-blocking diuretics are frequently used; and intervals between doses are often shorter, putting the kidneys under a continuous, chronic influence of the diuretic drug and preventing them from compensating for magnesium loss with drug-free or reduced-drug intervals.

The situation may be further aggravated by the presence of congestive heart failure. Diabetes mellitus and alcoholism may also contribute to urinary losses of magnesium.

Functions of Magnesium
Magnesium is an essential co-factor for about 300 different enzyme systems. It is of great importance for

splitting reactions and for transfer of phosphate groups; thus it is indispensable for the metabolism of adenosine triphosphate (ATP), which is involved in the utilization of glucose; the synthesis of fat, protein, nucleic acids, and co-enzyme systems; muscle contractions; and some energy-demanding transport systems. Hence, it is understandable that magnesium deficiency may present itself in many different way.

Magnesium Deficiency Symptoms

Symptoms attributable to magnesium deficiency are diversified. They occur principally in the nervous system, the skeletal muscles, the gastrointestinal tract, and the cardiovascular system.

Serum magnesium is not a reliable guide to the body content of magnesium, although a low serum magnesium concentration usually denotes a deficiency. Even with a low serum magnesium level, however, patients may be entirely free from symptoms of deficiency for considerable time. Then suddenly, without any noticeable change in disease activity, treatment regimen, or serum magnesium level, they may present with severe and sometimes life-threatening symptoms that will subside only after magnesium supplementation.

Symptoms associated with the central nervous system often begin with apathy, depression, or difficulty remembering and concentrating. In more severe deficiency, confusion or even hallucinations and paranoid ideas may be present, and eventually coma may occur.

Neuromuscular symptoms are often prominent in serious deficiency, and patients may present with tremor and muscle twitching. Muscular weakness is not uncommon. Tremor and fasciculation of the skeletal muscles, numbness, tingling, and cramps may occur, even in mild deficiency states. Uncoordinated movements, staggering walk, nystagmus, and tetany have been observed in more severe deficiency.

Gastrointestinal symptoms are common and consist of anorexia, loss of appetite, and indigestion. General abdominal pain, diarrhea, or constipation may occur.

Magnesium and Cardiac Dysrhythmias

Magnesium may influence the incidence of cardiac dysrhythmias in three different ways: by a direct effect, by an effect on potassium metabolism, and by interfering with calcium metabolism. The direct effects consists of a slowing of the sino-atrial node rate proportional to the serum magnesium concentration and independent of nerve impulses. Magnesium slows intra-atrial and intraventricular conduction, and there is prolongation of atrioventricular transition time. In animal experiments, the threshold for ventricular fibrillation has been shown to be elevated. These changes are essentially reversed when there is a magnesium deficiency. Accordingly, a higher incidence of atrial fibrillation, supraventricular tachycardia, serious ventricular ectopic beats, and ventricular tachycardia and fibrillation has been demonstrated in patients with concurrent acute myocardial infarction and hypomagnesemia.

Of paramount importance is the influence of magnesium on potassium metabolism. Magnesium has been shown to be an essential co-factor for sodium/potassium adenosinetriphosphatase, which provides the energy necessary to drive the sodium pump. When there is a magnesium deficiency, sodium cannot be transported from the cell and potassium brought into it in sufficient amounts. A new equilibrium is established with a low intracellular potassium content. In addition, magnesium has been shown to diminish potassium diffusion from the cells.

These changes disturb the ratio between intra and extracellular potassium concentration, which determines the resting membrane potential. A diminished intracellular potassium level increases automatism and excitability; concomitantly, the conduction of the impulse is slowed. This will set the stage for various types of cardiac dysrhythmias.

Low values for skeletal-muscle potassium have been demonstrated in patients on diuretic therapy and with a magnesium deficiency. The low muscle potassium supplementation alone, and there was no change in the frequency of ventricular ectopic beats. On the other hand, magnesium supplementation corrected the cellular potassium content, and, simultaneously, there was a significant (75 percent) decrease in the frequency of ventricular ectopic beats.

Magnesium is a physiological calcium antagonist. As mentioned earlier, a magnesium deficiency will result in a raised cellular sodium content. As the ratio rises between intra and extracellular sodium, the calcium-sodium countertransport mechanism is stimulated, leading to an increased cellular calcium content.

Magnesium Deficiency and Digitalis

The influence of magnesium on calcium metabolism is of particular importance when there is also digitalis therapy. A raised intracellular calcium level has been shown to produce repetitive digitalis toxic dysrhythmias. Furthermore, it has been demonstrated that magnesium deficiency results in an increased binding of digitalis to the myocardium. Significantly lower doses of digitalis were sufficent to produce life-threatening cardiac dysrhythmias in magnesium depleted dogs; these could be abolished by magnesium supplementation. In this context, the potassium status is also important. When dogs were rendered potassium deficient by 5 to 10 percent of their total body potassium, 60 percent lower doses of digitalis were once again able to produce life-threatening cardiac dysrhythmias. Taking notice that a magnesium deficiency, apart from depriving the heart of magnesium's inherent effects, may produce an intracellular potassium deficiency and a raised intracellular calcium level, it is not surprising that a great number of published case reports and small series studies have confirmed these theoretically expected effects of a combination of magnesium deficiency and digitalis medication in the clinical setting. In fact, this is the area in which most of the studies on the cardiac effects of magnesium deficiency have been published.

Diuretics - Potassium Supplementation

Supplementation usually succeeds in raising the serum potassium levels, but the effect on tissue potassium content is doubtful. About half of the studies performed claim an increase in the body content of potassium following supplementation, while the other half cannot demonstrate any such effect. The different outcome may be explained by differences in the patients' magnesium status in the different studies, since magnesium is necessary for the transportaion of potassium in the cells.

In studies in patients with diuretic-induced hypokalemia and a magnesium deficiency, it was possible to raise the serum potassium levels to normal by potassium supplementation, but there was no increase in muscle potassium content. In fact, a small decrease in muscle potassium content was recorded, which was probably due to increased aldosterone secretion induced by the raised serum potassium concentration.

In contrast, patients with an isolated potassium deficiency reacted favorably to potassium supplementation with both serum levels and skeletal-muscle potassium content. Thus, potassium supplementation may be entirely ineffective when there is a concomitant magnesium deficiency and may even lead to further potassium losses by inducing aldosterone secretion.

Magnesium and Arterial Hypertension

Some electrolytes, chiefly sodium and calcium, have been implicated in the genesis and maintenance of arterial hypertension. However, during recent years, attention has been drawn to the influence of magnesium status on blood pressure.

Populations in areas with a low magnesium content of soil and water have been found to have higher blood pressure than the inhabitants of areas with a normal or high magnesium content. Also, the incidence of ischemic heart disease and of sudden deaths has been reported to be higher in the low magnesium areas. Diuretic treated hypertensive patients with hypomagnesemia were found to require larger dosages of anti-hypertensive drugs than were needed by diuretic treated hypertensive patients with normal levels of magnesium.

In Finland, the simple addition of magnesium and potassium to table salt (with a concomitant reduction of sodium chloride to 45 percent) has resulted in a significant decrease in mean blood pressure of the population under study. This concept is of special interest, because the most commonly used drugs to control blood pressure are the conventional diuretics, which often involve a significant loss of magnesium from the body.

(Editor's Note: Three years ago, we developed a mineral combination salt which included potassium, sodium, magnesium, calcium, lysine, kelp, and silica. Instead of the reduction of sodium by 45% as the Finnish formula does, we have reduced the sodium by 65%, which should be even better.)

Thus, it is possible that diuretic-induced magnesium losses may adversely affect blood pressure control in the long run. It is also possible that increased doses of diuretics or of additional medication needed to adequately control blood pressure may be related to the negative influence of magnesium losses on blood pressure.

- 0 -

DANGERS OF DRUG TREATMENT

Much of the preceding research shows that dietary changes could eliminate high blood pressure in many hypertensive patients. In spite of that, the routine approach for many M.D.'s is to immediately start a patient on drugs usually without any recommendations for a dietary change. The dangerous side effects of the drugs used make this approach often more harmful to the patient than beneficial.

Diuretics, used to promote water elimination, are the drugs most commonly used. For instance, the thiazide diuretics such as Dyazide, Hydrodiuril, and Diuril have been shown to cause irregular heart rhythms. Dr. P. K. Whelton, who heads the British Medical Research Council trial of therapy, found that 33 percent of patients taking thiazide preparations had five irregular heart beats an hour in the daytime, and 20 percent of the whole group had them at night as well. Irregular heart beats often result when the blood potassium was reduced below normal. This occurs regularly in 10 to 15 percent of patients taking thiazide diuretics. Dr. Brian Holland studied twenty-one patients who had thiazide-induced low blood potassium levels and found that seven of them (33 percent) developed irregular rhythms.

In addition to causing irregular heart beat, thiazide diuretics have adverse effects on the metabolism. They have long been known to cause elevation of both the blood sugar and uric acid; the drugs will increase the severity of, or even cause, diabetes, gout or both. Thiazides also raise the blood cholesterol and triglycerides, which would negate their value as blood pressure lowering agents. High blood pressure is one of the three major risk factors for heart disease and strokes, elevated cholesterol and smoking being the other two. As Dr. Richard H. Grimm, of the Department of Medicine at the University of Minnesota Medical School, put it:

An increase is total serum cholesterol and low density lipo-protein fraction may increase coronary heart disease in patients treated with diuretics. This has special implications in hypertensive persons already at risk for atherosclerosis and coronary heart disease. Even a small average increase in these lipid fractions would have considerable public health import because of the millions taking these drugs. Consequently, it is important to clarify the relation between diuretics and blood lipid changes in a controlled trial.

Dr. Grimm's study was published in 1981 in the *Annals of Internal Medicine.* In that study, sixty men with mild high blood pressure - defined as diastolic pressure between 90 and 105 - were divided into groups receiving one or two commonly used diuretics or a placebo. Of those taking hydrochlorothiazide (the most commonly used thiazide), the cholesterol increased an average of 15 points. Of those taking chlorthalidone (another thiazide), the cholesterol increase was 19 points. Triglycerides also increased, as did the uric acid, with both thiazide diuretics. Dr. Grimm concluded that:

49.

. . . . the results of this study clearly show an adverse lipid metabolic affect for commonly used anti-hypertensive agents, the thiazide group of diuretics, known previously to affect glucose and uric acid mechanisms. This finding underscores the importance of continued research in the application of non-pharacological means to lower blood pressure, both as an adjunct to drugs and as primary treatment in a hygienic, preventive approach to blood pressure lowering.

Dr. Jan Drayen, of the University of California at Irvine, College of Medicine, has found that in many patients, the diuretics no longer bring down the blood pressure. Of fifty patients given thiazides, he found that 25 to 50 percent were non-responders. The reasons for the failure are probably due to the alteration of the other blood pressure agents produced by the body in response to the thiazide diuretic. For instance, as the diuretic lowers the blood pressure by causing sodium excretion, the body counters by increasing the production of two hormones, renin and aldosterone, which decreases sodium loss. Result: Increased Blood Pressure. The net result is that for many patients, these diuretics have no effect on the blood pressure, yet the patients suffer the significant dangers of the drugs themselves. And very often, other drugs are added to bring down the blood pressure.

NOTHING MORE DANGEROUS THAN DIURETICS

In an interview with Medical Tribune in 1984, Dr. David McCarron, from the University of Oregon, pointed out that "in terms of laboratory tests, there is no single agent that the physician can prescribe that has more adverse effect than a thiazide diuretic." No one study has produced convincing evidence that using thiazide diuretics reduces the death rate of the mildly hypertensive patient with blood pressure ranging from 140/90 to 160/100. In fact, a large scale government funded **study** called the Multiple Risk Factor Intervention Trial (MRFIT) found that **the mortality rate was actually higher in a group of hypertensive patients that received aggressive treatment compared to a group of hypertensive patients that received no treatment or less aggressive approaches.** Another study by Dr. Anders Helgeland, of Oslo, Norway, demonstrated that the incidences of **sudden death among patients with mild hypertension, who were treated with hydrochlorothiazide, was three times that of the control group not treated with the drug.**

ALARMING STUDY

A particularly alarming study was published by Dr. Gary Cutter, head of the biometry division and associate professor of biostatistics at the University of Alabama. In a series of 5,000 patients who had undergone a cardiac catheterization and angiogram during the years 1970 to 1978 and who had been followed annually, **those taking diuretics had a 1.4 time greater death rate than those not taking diuretics.** Also, those taking diuretics had 1.5 times greater risk of death from cardiac disease. He did not specify the type of diuretic that was utilized, but the thiazide diuretics are by far the most commonly used.

Considering all the potential harm of thiazide diuretics, a few physicians are now sounding the alarm. Dr. Edward D. Freis, of the Veterans Administration Medical Center in Washington, D.C., published an editorial in the *New England Journal of Medicine* entitled "Should Mild Hypertenstion Be Treated?" In it, he challenged the concept of drug therapy for mildly hypertensive patients, pointing out that the treatment could be worse than the disease.

I know you are going to look at some of these facts and ask youself how could your doctor continue to prescribe these medicines if he know what is being presented here? Doctoring becomes a routine job after awhile and the routine has been established so long that it becomes automatic. The patient is going to have to force the change, the doctor never will.

BLOOD PRESSURE MONITORING AT HOME DURING PREGNANCY

A three year study of 59 chronically hypertensive pregnant women concluded that, with proper instruction, such patients can reliably monitor their own blood pressure at home. According to researchers from the Ohio State University and the University of Michigan, self-monitoring of blood pressure during pregnancy has a number of advantages for both patient and physician. Chief among these advantages is that self-monitoring enables the patients to become more actively involved in their own health care. Patients also gain a better appreciation of the effects of rest, various activities, and stress on their blood pressure.

For example, women were asked to take their blood pressure before and after resting on their side each day. The lower blood pressure readings patients obtained after resting reinforced the need for this daily therapeutic rest period better than any doctor could.

Blood pressure measurements taken at home varied greatly from those taken in the office, as has been observed in other studies. The researchers, therefore, asserted that home monitoring provides the clinician with valuable information for making decisions as to the necessity of treatment. It is a recognized, but overlooked, fact that pressures are often elevated when taken in the doctor's office. How many individuals are taking medication for a condition that only exisits temporarily in their doctor's office?

ALCOHOL AND BLOOD PRESSURE

British researchers have demonstrated that moderate alcohol consumption raises blood pressure in patients with essential hypertension. Sixteen patients who regularly drank moderate amounts of alcohol (up to 3 oz. per day) were admitted to the hospital and studied for seven days. All anti-hypertensive drugs were stopped two weeks earlier.

Eight subjects continued their regular drinking for three days and abstained from alcohol for the next four days. Systolic and diastolic blood pressure rose in five and three patients, respectively, when alcohol was used; and fell in seven and six patients, respectively, when it was stopped.

The remaining eight patients abstained from alcohol for the first three days and resumed their regular drinking for the last four days. Systolic and diastolic blood pressures fell in five and four patients, respectively, when they abstained from alcohol; and rose in seven and all eight patients, respectively, 48 hours after drinking was resumed. The "slow pressure" effect of delayed reaction of alcohol suggested by the latter finding may explain why increases in blood pressure have not been documented in acute studies. If the patients had been followed up for two or more days, they may have found the same results as this.

WHAT DOES SIMON SAY?

The following direct lifting of copy from *Physician and Patient* in their "Letters to the Editor Department" clearly gives you an idea of the frustration the average doctor faces when it comes to treating high blood pressure. This is a direct word for word quotation from the May, 1984 issue of *Physicians and Patient* magazine.

"Ready, hypertensives? Here we go! Simon says, put down your salt shaker. Simon says, pick it up. Simon says, take your medicine. Simon says, don't take it. Simon says, take it.
Recognize the game? It's called "Treating Hypertension." Physicians and patients are the contestants, and Simon is the state of the art medical wisdom.
The stakes are very high. If you win, you beat hypertension. Then you possibly avoid a heart attack or stroke. If you lose, you could have these problems, and perhaps die. On the other hand, you can win and still have a heart attack; in fact, winning might even make it more likely. You might also develop gout, impotency, or a lot of other fun things. Great game, isn't it?
Oh - there's one more monkey wrench. The rules change whenever Simon says. Unfortunately, Simon has been saying a lot lately.
We're not talking about the malignant hypertension that pushes the optic disc through the iris, or even the mod-

erate hypertension that makes us take two or three steps of stepped-care in one leap. No, we're talking mild hypertension. The 90-104 diastolics. (Our old friends - the rent payers.) This is the hypertension we see most often and still can't get a handle on.

Drug companies are avid watchers of this game since they provide some of the most important equipment. Their representatives often ask me, "Doctor, how do *you* treat hypertension?" I never seem to have the answer they're looking for: If I say start with diuretics, they tell me Europeans use beta-blockers or central agents as monotherapy; if I say start with beta-blockers or central agents, they tell me diuretics are still the cornerstone of stepped-care. Usually I laugh and tell them my approach depends on the last thing I've read. They think I'm kidding.

Life was simple after HDFP. The Hypertension Detection and Follow-Up Program was the five year study that told us in 1979 that *all* levels of hypertension benefited from treatment. Even people with mild high blood pressure given special attention the "stepped-care" group had decreased cardiovascular mortality. This was a dramatic finding, since perhaps 70% of all hypertensives are mild, and we could, therefore, offer them a statistically significant reduction in their incidence of cardiac and cerebral events. How nice to have been able to leave the limbo of "borderline hypertension," the land of 140/90. The 90's do better at 86 or 84, so let's treat them.

Then came MRFIT in September, 1982, and suddenly special intervention wasn't so special anymore. The Multiple Rish Factor Intervention Trial showed that some mild hypertensives with resting ECG abnormalities actually had *more* deaths than those who supposedly were treated less aggressively. This raised lots of questions. Are diuretics harmful for some patients? Were there problems with electrolytes or lipids? MRFIT demanded another serious look at treatment philosophy.

A special issue of the *Annals of Internal Medicine* in May, 1983 dealt with nutrition and blood pressure control. Dr. Norman Kaplan, from the University of Texas, wrote the lead-off article. (I first saw him in a medical school education film giving a "diuretics for the rest of your life" speech to a hypertensive woman.) In the *Annals* article, he talks about re-defining high blood pressure with a detailed benefit risk analysis. What are the risks of long term anti-hypertensive therapy? Apart from potential electrolyte, glucose, lipid and uric acid disturbances, how about the effects of turning an asymptomatic person into a "patient," one who squirms in the waiting room, catecholamines working overtime, wondering if the "silent killer" is advancing.

Kaplan suggests putting high blood pressure into a context, so that if glucose, cholesterol, and ECG are normal and the person doesn't smoke, isolated hypertension might not be so much of a threat. For such a patient, it might be more appropriate to start with careful surveillance instead of medical treatment and trying non-drug therapies - weight reduction, relaxation, exercise. (Simon now says, *don't* treat the 90-diastolics.) Other articles in this Annals issue explores the notion that salt restriction may be effective in perhaps only 30% of all hypertensives. One article suggests that salt restriction can actually hurt some people. (Simon says, bring back the salt shaker?)

And it hasn't stopped there. Other articles have appeared preaching the alternate message - no salt and stepped-care for mild hypertension. Still more papers question that. On and on. Simon says this. Simon says that.

Two months ago I'm treating 140/90, now I'm letting 150/94 slide! *Hypertension isn't labile. The treatment is!*

What are we supposed to do, we family docs in the trenches, while the generals debate data base and double blind? I knew that uncertainty came with the territory, I didn't know it **was** the territory.

So here we are, poised after acting out our last set of instructions, hoping, at least, that we do no harm. As we hold our position, we wonder. We pray. We wait to hear what Simon will say."

Richard Donze, D.O.
Family Health Service
Methodist Hospital, Philadelphia

IN SUMMARY

There can be no question that medicine is not a true science, that's why it's called a "practice." The only historical fact that has been constant in medicine is the fact that it changes its opinion on therapy every so often and the new approach could be diametrically opposed to the preceding therapy. One very aggravating historical fact is that change is always opposed by the older doctors who usually also control medicine. Because of this, the average new idea takes from 20 to 50 years for the profession to accept.

As an example, a five year study of over 1,800 women, indicated that lumpectomy was successful or more so than total mastectomy. The study was completed well over eight years ago and even today, many surgeons are still taking a "let's wait and see" attitude and going ahead and doing their radical mastectomies. Nutrition has been shoved aside in medicine probably because it doesn't have the glamour that other therapies do. On a more basic note, it also doesn't have the profit in it that other practices do.

Recent material has been presented that gives a clear indication that hypertension should be treated first with nutritional substances before drugs are used, which often have more serious side effects than the hypertension itself.

The evidence presented in this book makes it clear that one should consider carefully the alternatives to medication for high blood pressure. We have only presented a small portion of the many studies linking biochemical changes to this condition. All the dozens of studies in which meditation, exercise, biofeedback, acupuncture and acupressure, chiropractic adjustments, herbal use and other methodologies were used successfully are not even mentioned. In trying to keep this book to a readable size, I have concentrated on emphasizing the vacillation of the medical profession in treating the condition of hypertension, while at the same time exploring the three nutritional elements which could potentially be used in place of any harmful drugs. Let's review what we did say:

1. A variety of conditions can contribute to true hypertension, including smoking, stress, liver or kidney disease, atherosclerosis and certain tumors.

2. Oral and/or intravenous chelation may have a beneficial effect on atherosclerosis, reducing it to where it is not a factor in hypertension.

3. Doctors vacillate as to the treatment of high blood pressure, not only as to the kinds of drugs that should be used, but also as to just what reading constitutes high blood pressure.

4. The most common drugs used - the diuretic thiazides - are among the most toxic drugs which doctors can prescribe and often produce such disorders as impotency, gout, cholesterol and triglyceride increase, irregular heart beat, diabetes, three time greater risk of sudden death, 1.5 times greater risk of death from cardiovascular disease, and others.

5. If you suspect high blood pressure, invest in a Baumanometer of other blood pressure taking devise and monitor your blood pressure on a regular daily basis at home. Many individuals are treated for "white coat" hypertension, which only occurs in the doctor's office.

6. The use of calcium supplements can be effective in up to 50% of the hypertensives now treated with drugs.

7. Ample evidence exists to indicate that potassium deficiency is a far more critical factor in hypertension than sodium excess. In certain tests, the addition of potassium was dramatic in preventing either stroke or cardiac trauma from high blood pressure, acting in some way to change the fragility of the artery for the better.

8. Magnesium, a critical mineral in the over three hundred biochemical reactions in the body, is essential to get potassium into the cell. The use of potassium supplements will often raise a low serum potassium, but tissue levels of potassium will remain low in the absence of magnesium. Arrythmias and rapid heart beats could be due to a magnesium/potassium deficiency.

9. Lead will deposit in the calcium storehouse during a calcium deficiency. There has been a determination that a previously considered innocuous amount of lead will product hypertension with less lead necessary to produce hypertension as one ages.

10. Ingestion of alcohol has a direct negative

effect on hypertension.

CONCLUSION

The use of alternative approaches to the problems of hypertension should always be considered first. The use of calcium-magnesium-potassium formulas as an alternative to present drug treatment of hypertension should probably be considered by every physician who works with patients. There are few, if any, possible side effects and the literature is quite convincing that there is merit in such an approach.

Perhaps, as in Finland, we should use a substitute for regular sodium chloride salt. It need not be totally devoid of sodium, just modified by other minerals to create a physiological formula.

Exercise and reduction of stress play a part in any healthy lifestyle, but do more for the hypertensive than those who do not have high blood pressure.

Quitting smoking is an essential change for anyone who has a blood pressure problem

If your physician wishes to furnish you with drugs for your hypertension, you might consider handing him a copy of this book and request that he treat you first with these suggestions. If he is insulted, you probably have the wrong doctor, and would do well to find another. Always remember - it is your body!

ORAL CHELATION FORMULA

Vitamin A (Betacarotene)	15,000 IU
Vitamin D (Fish Liver Oil)	240 IU
Vitamin E (d-alpha tocopherol)	360 IU
Vitamin C (ca. asc. & asc. acid)	1,800 mg
Vitamin B-1	100 mg
Vitamin B-2	30 mg
Vitamin B-6	90 mg
Niacin	60 mg
Pantothenic Acid	100 mg
Vitamin B-12	150 mcg
Folic Acid	240 mcg
Biotin	60 mcg
Choline	450 mg
Inositol	60 mg
PABA	90 mg
Calcium	240 mg
Magnesium	300 mg
Iodine	135 mcg
Iron	4.5 mg
Copper	150 mcg
Zinc	15 mg
Potassium	240 mg
Manganese	6 mg
Chromium	120 mcg
Cysteine	450 mg
Methionine	120 mcg
Germanium	25 mcg
Selenium	120 mcg
Ginko Biloba	30 mg
L-Carnitine	50 mg
Bilberry Extract	25 mg
DiMethyl Glycine	50 mg
Hawthorne Berry	15 mg
Thymus	50 mg
EPA/DHA	25 mg
Co Q-10	10 mg
Chondroitin Sulfate	50 mg

MORE FORMULAS

Calcium - Magnesium - Potassium - Boron

Calcium	675 mg
Magnesium	450 mg
Potassium	297 mg
Boron	3 mg

I like this formula because it make physiological sense. The boron is a comparative newcomer to the nutritional world but it greatly enhances the tissue uptake of calcium as well as bing a hormoe synergist.

Seasoning Salt

Potassium
Sodium
Calcium
Magnesium
Kelp
Lysine

This tastes good on any food, answers your need for a salty taste and yet doesn't upset the sodium/potassium balance. You also get a little extra lysine, a real necessary amino acid.

ANTI-HYPERTENSIVE DIET

Please do not feel that you are bound to a tasteless diet just because you may have high blood pressure. As we have presented in this book, there is evidence that a very low sodium diet may be injurious to some. So the Seasoning Salt that we recommend, can be used freely. I feel that it is more important to know what you can eat than to give a list of undesirable foods. The following are very general guidelines, but constitute a good approach to social eating with a purpose.

1. Do eat 4 cupfuls of vegetables per day. Get as much variety as you can. They may be partially cooked or eaten raw, a 50/50 mix of cooked and raw is good.

2. Do use olive, peanut or canola oil for all cooking purposes. **Never** use the poly-unsaturated oils so heavily touted.

3. Do use butter when necessary - **never** use margarine under any circumstances.

4. Reduce the amount of fat in your diet, but there is no reason to totally eliminate it, since food will taste terrible without it.

5. Do eat fish at least twice weekly. Do rotate your meats (if you consume meat) so that you use a variety of fowl and a variety of meat. Cut off all fat possible.

6. Reduce the use of refined sugar products to an absolute minimum.

7. Stay away from processed, smoked, compressed meats. They are loaded with fat and salt.

8. Refrain from alcoholic beverages.

9. Refrain from coffee and tea (except herbal).

10. Read labels and look for MSG (mono sodium glutamate), a flavor enhancer that causes an allergic reaction in some and that raises blood pressure. You'll be amazed at how many foods contain it.

Now that isn't too bad, is it? A wide variety of good foods exist in the marketplace if we will only shop for them. Many of us haven't tasted half of the vegetables on the shelves. Why not try one new vegetable each week, you don't have to like them all, but you might surprise yourself as to how many you will.

Fruits are fine for snacks or desserts, but most fruit juices and some vegetable juices are extremely high in sugar, which is not desirable.

Drink lots of water, it gives your body a chance to cleanse itself. But don't drink the tap water, get a filter or buy pure water.

Side Effects of Blood Pressure Medication

I am often requested to give information as to side effects of the various medications used by those with high blood pressure. It is quite impossible to list all the various prescriptions that might be written by a doctor for hypertension, but the following are some of the most commonly used blood pressure medicines and their side effects.

Aldactazide A "Warning" box appears right below the listing of this drug. It states, **"Spironolactone, an ingredient of Aldactazide, has been shown to be a turmorigen in chronic toxicity studies in rats. Aldactazide should only be used for those conditions described under *Indications and Usage*. Unnecessary use of this drug should be avoided."**

(Editor's Note: If you are taking this drug on the advise of your doctor, ask him if he is aware that it can cause tumors and whether or not it is the only medication which is possible in your condition. Following the advise in this booklet might offer you a non-toxic alternative without medication.)

Side Effects: Gynecomastia (Enlargement of breasts) Agranulocytosis (an acute febrile condition marked by severe depression of the granulocyte-producing bone marrow and by prostration, chills, swollen neck, and sore throat sometimes with local ulceration and believed to be basically a response to the side effect of certain drugs) Decreased Glucose Tolerance, Gout, Cramping,

Diarrhea, Drowsiness, Lethargy, Headache, Rash, Mental Confusion, Fever, Loss of Balance, Inability to Achieve or Maintain an Erection, Irregular Mense, Amenorrhea, Gastric Bleeding, Jaundice, Restlessness, Ulcers, Carcinoma of the Breast, Post-Menopausal Bleeding (How's that for Russian Roulette?)

Aldomet This drug has as its active ingredient methyldopa, whose action is to cause a net reduction in the tissue concentration of serotonin, dopamine, norepinephrine and epinephrine.
Side Effects: Headaches, Dizziness, Light-headedness, Diarrhea, Constipation, Loss of Appetite, Blurred or Distorted Vision, Dry Mouth, Dry Skin, Decreased Sexual Interest or Ability
Warning: With prolongedmethyldopa therapy, 10 to 20 percent of patients develop a positive direct Coombs test which usually occurs between 6 and 12 months of methyldopa therapy. This may be associated with hemolytic anemia, which could lead to potentially fatal complications. One cannot predict which patient with a positive direct Coombs test may develop hemolytic anemia.
Rarely fatal hepatic necrosis has been reported after use of methyldopa. These hepatic changes may represent hypersensitivity reactions. Periodic determination of hepatic (liver) function should be done, particularly during the first 6 to 12 weeks of therapy or if an unex-

plained fever arises.

Aldoril   A combination of methyldopa and
hydrochlorthiazide, this medicine works like "Aldomet",
but has a diuretic combined with it. It is often used
when the doctor does not know what the cause of the
hypertension is, so he uses two drugs with different
actions. The diuretic action reduces both the sodium
and the potassium levels in the body and can cause some
problems unrelated to direct side effects. Use with
caution in renal (kidney) disease or dysfunction. In
patients with renal disease, thiazides may precipitate
azotemia. Cumulative effects may occur. Thiazides
should be used with caution by people with impaired
hepatic (liver) function or progressive liver disease,
since minor alterations in electrolyte or fluid balance
may occur in patients with a history of allergy or
bronchial asthma. Activation or exacerbation of lupus
erythematosis has been reported.
Side Effects: Headaches, Dizziness, Lightheadedness,
Diarrhea, Constipation, Loss of Appetite, Increased
Sensitivity to the Sun, Increased/Frequent Urination,
Decreased Sexual Interest or Ability, Muscle and Joint
Pain, Amenorrhea, Rash, Parkinsonism, Bell's Palsy,
Decreased Mental Acuity, Psychic Distrubances,
Depression.

Cardizem A calcium channel blocker or calcium
antagonist, cardizem lowers blood pressure by inhibiting

the introduction of calcium into the smooth muscle fibers of the heart and the blood vessels. This reduces heart rate and causes a relaxation of the blood vessel. This is a very well tolerated drug, with considerably less side effects than most hypotensive drugs. The following are the most common side effects and the percentage of patients who might experience them: Edema (2.4%), Headache (2.1%), Nausea (1.9%), Dizziness (1.5%), Rash (1.3%), Weakness (1.2%)

Dyazide Contains hydrochlorothiazide as in "Aldoril", plus another diuretic called triamterene. The triamterene is similar in effect to hydrochlorothiazide in that it promotes the excretion of sodium, but triamterene is far more sparing of potassium than hydrochlorothiazide is.
Side Effects: Anaphylaxis, Rash, Arrythmia, Postural Hypotension, Diabetes, Mellitus, Jaundice, Pancreatitis, Nausea and Vomiting, Diarrhea, Constipation, Kidney Failure, Leukopenia, Muscle Cramps, Weakness, Fatigue, Headaches, Impotency, Loss of Appetite, Increased Sensitivity to the Sun, Blurred or Distorted Vision

Lopressor The major ingredient here is metoprolol tartrate, a selective beta-adrenoreceptor blocking agent, combined with hydrochlorothiazide. We already know a lot about hydrochlorothiazide, so let's concentrate on the "beta-blocker." The term relates to the ability of this drug to block the neural impulse which causes certain muscle activity. In this case, it causes relaxation of the smooth muscle fibers of the heart and blood vessels. This produces reduction of heart rate and efficiency and should never be used with a patient who has congestive heart failure. **Patients with brochospastic disordes should not, in general, receive beta-blockers.** Fatigue and/or lethargy and flu syndrome have been reported in 10 out of 100 patients. Depression has been reported in 5 out of 100 patients. Mental confusion and short term memory loss are also a frequent side effect. Add these to all the side effects of hydrochlorothiazide, as listed previously, and you have what appears to be a drug which should be used most cautiously.

Tenormin This drug is a pure beta-blocker without combination. A major warning on the use of this medicine involves termination of use. If a patient has coronary artery disease, the abrupt discontinuation of Tenormin may result in acute angina attacks and myocardial infaction (heart attack). Severe arrythmias have also been reported.
Side Effects: Fever, Sore Throat, Muscle Aches, Larygospasm, Respiratory Distress, Mental Depression Progressing to Catatonia, Visual Disturbances, Hallucinations, Short Term Memory Loss

Inderal A beta-blocker, similar to "Tenormin"
Diuril Hydrochlorthiazide, similar to "Dyazide"
Isoptin A calcium blocker, similar to "Cardizem"

REACH FOR LIFE
HEALTH
SPA

A Luxurious Facility at Economy Prices
12 day programs starting at $1725

Supervised by
Kurt W. Donsbach, D.C., N.D., Ph.D.
H. Rudolph Alsleben, M.D., D.O., Ph.D.

Complete Physical Examination
Blood and Urine Analysis
Bio-Ionization Analysis
Nutrition Counseling
Chelation
Herbal Body Wraps
Pain Relief Therapy
Facial Rejuvenation
Live Cell Therapy
Juice Fasting
Massage and Physiotherapy

For Further Information Call: 1-800-359-6547

If you liked this booklet, you will probably enjoy some of the other writings of these two doctors:

- **Arthritis**
- **Candidiasis & Chronic Fatigue**
- **Heart Disease/Oral Chelation**
- **High Blood Pressure**
- **Allergies and Stress**
- **Hypoglycemia & Diabetes**
- **Hysterectomy & Menopause**
- **Oxygen Therapy ($O_2O_2O_2$)**
- **Water**
- **Wholistic Cancer Therapy**
- **Get Well Through Self-Detox**
- **Acne, Eczema, Psoriasis**
- **Overweight & Underweight**
- **Interpreting Blood & Urine Tests**
- **Live Cell Therapy**
- **Acupressure & Reflex Massage**
- **Alfalfa, Bee Pollen, Ginseng**
- **Neg. Ions, Ozone & Clean Air**
- **Non-Invasive Testing**

NOTES

NOTES

NOTES

NOTES

NOTES

EMBRACING WHOLISTIC HEALTH

by Kurt W. Donsbach, D.C., N.D., Ph.D.

CLARIFYING THE BODY-MIND-SPIRIT CONNECTION
in
CANCER • ARTHRITIS • CANDIDIASIS
HEART DISEASE • MULTIPLE SCLEROSIS

Explicit treatment protocols from the world famous natural healing institutions - Hospital Santa Monica, Hospital St. Augustine and Institut Santa Monica

You can order this 300 page profusely illustrated manual by checking with your local health food store or calling 1-800-423-7662. Total Cost: $14.95. Dr. Donsbach feels this is his best work yet. You should have this book on your shelf to help you answer health questions that may come up. It is the best review of the application and merits of wholistic health philosophy available today.